How to Get Tenure

Helping assistant professors and pre-tenure faculty balance competing obligations in teaching, research, and service, this comprehensive book explores the challenging path toward tenure. Drawing from research literature on faculty development, pedagogy, and psychology, *How to Get Tenure* covers topics such as productivity, research agendas, publication, service, and preparing a dossier. Whether read from beginning to end or used as a reference, this book provides clear, concrete, and accessible advice on the most effective and efficient strategies for navigating the inherent ambiguity of the tenure process, tackling the challenges and complexity of the tenure track, and building a strong case for tenure.

Michael S. Harris is an Associate Professor of Higher Education, and Director of the Center for Teaching Excellence (CTE) at Southern Methodist University, USA.

How to Get Tenure

Strategies for Successfully
Navigating the Process

Michael S. Harris

Routledge
Taylor & Francis Group

NEW YORK AND LONDON

First published 2019
by Routledge
711 Third Avenue, New York, NY 10017

and by Routledge
2 Park Square, Milton Park, Abingdon, Oxon, OX14 4RN

Routledge is an imprint of the Taylor & Francis Group, an informa business

Library of Congress Cataloging-in-Publication Data
Names: Harris, Michael S., author.
Title: How to get tenure : strategies for successfully navigating the
process / by Michael S. Harris.
Description: New York : Routledge, 2018. | Includes bibliographical
references.
Identifiers: LCCN 2018004597| ISBN 9780815380900 (hbk) |
ISBN 9780815380931 (pbk) | ISBN 9781351211581 (ebk) |
ISBN 9781351211550 (mobi/kindle) | ISBN 9781351211574
(Web PDF) | ISBN 9781351211567 (ePub)
Subjects: LCSH: College teachers—Tenure—United States—Handbooks,
manuals, etc.
Classification: LCC LB2335.7 .H37 2018 | DDC 378.1/214—dc23
LC record available at https://lccn.loc.gov/2018004597

ISBN: 978-0-8153-8090-0 (hbk)
ISBN: 978-0-8153-8093-1 (pbk)
ISBN: 978-1-351-21158-1 (ebk)

Typeset in Perpetua and Bell Gothic
by Florence Production Ltd, Stoodleigh, Devon, UK

Visit the eResources: www.routledge.com/9780815380931

Dedication

For Suzette—my partner in tenure *and* life.

Contents

Preface

It was about 2 o'clock on a Friday afternoon when I decided to stand up and stretch my legs. I have always enjoyed working in the office on Fridays because it tends to be quiet and I can be productive, and I had spent the last couple of hours editing a manuscript that I needed to finish. I walked down the hall to the department office to check my mailbox. I rarely received much more than junk mail, but checking gave me an excuse to get out of my office for a few minutes and say hello to the department administrative assistants before returning to work for another couple of hours. This time, my mailbox was not holding junk mail; instead, there was an envelope on the University's official stationery that noted it was from the Provost's office. I immediately knew what was inside. While the earlier stages of the tenure review process had meant I was getting regular updates about my progress, once my tenure file went to the university level it was almost like falling into a black hole. I knew I would hear at some point before the end of April, but I had no idea when to expect *the letter* to arrive.

I was now holding in my hand an envelope that would have profound implications for my career as well as my personal life. Everything I had worked for in the last six years—longer than that, really—came down to the evaluation and decision contained in this letter. Having received positive reviews earlier in the process, I was confident that this decision would be in my favor, but you can never really know until you read the fate you have been assigned. I started to open the envelope immediately but quickly decided that, if the news was not good, I did not want to be standing in the middle of the department. I started walking back down the hall, but about halfway back to my office the suspense became too much for me and I opened the envelope. It was a formal letter on stationery signed by the provost. Yes, this was indeed my tenure letter. I read the first line: "After a careful review of your promotion and tenure file, I am pleased to inform you that you will be awarded tenure and promotion to the rank of associate professor."

I had done it. The long hours, the stress, the hard work had paid off. I was a tenured associate professor. It is hard to describe the emotions of receiving that letter. On one hand, I was confident that I had done what had been asked and felt

I deserved the investment the university was placing in me. On the other hand, the tenure process could be vague and, in many ways, I never fully knew where I stood. I was relieved. I was grateful. I was happy. This was the longest and hardest I had ever worked for anything in my life, up to that point or since. Fortunately, my story had a positive ending.

However, this outcome was neither guaranteed nor without challenges. At one point, I was not sure if I wanted to continue and even interviewed for a non-faculty job. As I look back on my pre-tenure years, I remember feeling the uncertainty, apprehension, and lack of confidence in my ability to succeed as a faculty member. Yet, I also know I had some significant advantages. My area of expertise and research is in the organization and governance of higher education, and I study colleges and universities, faculty, and administrators as part of my research agenda. Even with all these advantages, tenure was intense and, at times, a real struggle. In talking with my fellow higher education colleagues, we would often say, "We're scholars of this stuff! If this is hard for us, what about those faculty who are going through the same process as we are, but without the scholarly background of higher education and knowledge of the tenure process?"

Years later, I find myself directing my university's teaching center and thinking about the current state of pre-tenure faculty. As part of my role, I spend a lot of time meeting with, mentoring, and discussing tenure issues with assistant professors across campus. Through these discussions, I hear about the many challenges pre-tenure faculty face today. Some of these are the same as those I faced, while others are different given the current context of higher education. In this book, I hope to bring together my experience as a researcher of higher education, as a faculty member who survived the tenure process, and as someone who works regularly with assistant professors. My goal is to provide strategies and information based on the most recent literature on faculty and higher education, in order for pre-tenure faculty to be successful in their pursuit of tenure. There are multiple books on tenure that provide advice and suggestions for pre-tenure faculty. These resources can be extremely beneficial, and I reference many of them throughout the chapters here. As a scholar of higher education, however, I also realize that many of these books fail to leverage the growing higher education research base to benefit faculty across a variety of disciplines on campus.

ABOUT THIS BOOK

The tenure process can vary dramatically based on the type of institution (i.e. a teaching or research university), the nature of the discipline, the culture of the academic department, and personal circumstances. I have written this book to be broadly applicable to faculty pursuing tenure in any college or university. Where differences may occur based on particular circumstances, I note these and provide some ideas for the reader to determine what is most appropriate in a particular case. The examples used throughout this book are drawn from research conducted in many different contexts, as well as from my own experiences. As the reader, you will be best able to apply the ideas in this book when considering your local context and the peculiarities of your own path to tenure.

This book also comes from the perspective of someone offering advice to pre-tenure faculty going through the tenure process. Thus, while the strategies and advice within these pages are directed toward them, the research and lessons throughout may also prove beneficial to department chairs, deans, faculty developers, and others who mentor assistant professors. For these readers, the ideas and concepts here can provide additional information or recommendations to aid in formal and informal mentorship. Even better, pre-tenure faculty and senior colleagues can read the book together to spark a productive dialogue about how to successfully navigate the tenure process in specific circumstances unique to individual disciplines and institutions.

I have designed *How to Get Tenure* to be read from beginning to end or used as a reference manual. For graduate students and new tenure track professors, I recommend working through the book in order to gain a full appreciation of the process that you are about to undergo. For experienced pre-tenure faculty or mentors, you may find that referencing particular chapters will be helpful in answering specific questions. I have identified areas in the book that warrant additional thought and reflection. The "Pause and Reflect" prompts will encourage you to think more deeply and question your own practices. Moreover, I included a number of worksheets throughout the book to assist with applying the strategies and ideas presented. In addition to their inclusion here, the worksheets are also available for download from the book's site on Routledge's webpage at www.routledge.com/9780815380931. This book is broken into three parts to guide you through the aspects of the tenure process. Part I provides a background for understanding the work and productivity necessary for faculty to succeed on the tenure track. Chapter 1 considers the current environment for tenure and sets the stage for understanding the tenure process. Through a discussion of the history of tenure and the current state of tenure in higher education, the chapter provides a foundation for understanding the subsequent chapters. In Chapter 2, I examine faculty work in the context of knowledge work, technology, and competing priorities. The chapter begins by providing a strategic orientation considering deep work, goal setting, and focus for pre-tenure faculty. Next, the chapter offers specific tactical approaches such as managing email, setting a weekly schedule, and budgeting goals. The chapter's goal is to reorient faculty to consider academic work through the tenure lens and provide specific approaches to accomplish all types of faculty work effectively and efficiently.

Part II explores the three primary aspects of faculty work considered as part of tenure at most institutions (scholarship and academic publishing, teaching, and service). Chapter 3 discusses scholarship and academic publishing, critical elements in nearly every tenure case. I begin by discussing the importance of academic publishing and developing a research agenda to establish an academic career timeline. After this discussion, I turn to consider specific aspects of research activities that can cause challenges for pre-tenure faculty, including grants and contracts, collaborating with colleagues and students, and finding time to write each day.

Chapter 4 provides an approach to teaching that maximizes student learning while emphasizing efficiency during the years on the tenure clock. Specifically, I introduce readers to the benefits of active learning for both students and faculty. The chapter discusses key teaching issues such as class policies, creating inclusive classrooms, grading, and student evaluations to provide preparation for teaching that will benefit students and improve a candidate's case for tenure.

In Chapter 5, I discuss the complicated nature of service. Many pre-tenure faculty struggle with service as an aspect of faculty work that takes up a great deal of time yet receives little consideration in the tenure decision. I outline types of service and how they are evaluated during tenure review. The chapter also helps pre-tenure faculty decide when to say "yes" to service, as well as how to say "no" well.

To conclude the book, Part III discusses the process of being considered for tenure, preparing the tenure dossier, and what happens afterwards. Chapter 6 discusses how the process works and the key decision points along the way. Specifically, the chapter examines tenure criteria, managing professional image, and the important constituencies for every tenure candidate. The chapter describes in detail how to prepare the tenure dossier and personal statement, as well as how to consider potential external reviewers in creating the important documents for tenure committees to review.

After receiving tenure, newly minted associate professors should celebrate and think about the next stage of their academic careers. In Chapter 7, I encourage tenured faculty to think about new research projects and how to now take chances with their careers while looking ahead to promotion to full professor. I also encourage tenured faculty to pay their success forward by supporting pre-tenure faculty and acknowledging the support they received along the path to tenure. By describing life after tenure, this chapter hopefully provides a goal to strive toward and a plan for faculty to leverage tenure to serve others.

My approach throughout this book builds on my basic belief that everyone who has the ability to land a tenure track assistant professorship has the ability to achieve tenure, although this outcome is not guaranteed. *How to Get Tenure* provides information, strategies, and tactics for pre-tenure faculty to know exactly how to get tenure. I hope you, the pre-tenure reader, will apply these lessons and work to learn about the tenure process just as you work on other aspects of academic work such as scholarship, teaching, and service. Ultimately, becoming a scholar of the tenure process is one of the best ways to clarify ambiguity, manage expectations, and establish a career that meets, or exceeds, the tenure requirements at your institution.

Acknowledgments

First, I must express my gratitude to the members of my weekly Education Policy and Leadership writing group. Throughout the process of writing this book, I have been encouraged by the work ethic of my department colleagues who have pushed me to keep up with their talents, intellectual curiosity, and rigor. In addition, they have provided thoughtful advice and feedback throughout the writing process that has undoubtedly made this book much better than it would have been otherwise. Thank you to Dominique Baker, Sondra Barringer, Dan Berebitsky, Denisa Gándara, Alex Pavlakis, Meredith Richards, and Ashley Tull.

Karri Holley has been a trusted friend and colleague since we were both on the tenure-track together and read early versions of many chapters in this book. Karri's thoughtfulness, editorial suggestions, and encouragement continues to improve my work immensely.

My thanks to Brian Bourke, Milan Sevak, and Matt Stone for their insights on various chapters as well as to the three outside reviewers who likewise improved the book. Additionally, I appreciate the support of Kiersten Ferguson, Stephanie Knight, Dawson Orr, and Paige Ware.

I am grateful to my colleagues in the SMU Center for Teaching Excellence: Jordan Morrison, Addy Tolliver, and Doug Wilson. Each supported my necessary absences while writing this book and each are dedicated to supporting faculty on our campus. Former Associate Provost Linda Eads, who asked me to direct the Center, supported me and served as a valuable mentor in learning academic administration.

One of the great joys of faculty life is getting to work with supremely talented students. Molly Ellis, my long-time research assistant, went above and beyond the call to help see this book to fruition. I value her thoughtfulness, insights, and her ability to know what I am thinking often before I do. Casey Africano, one of our higher education master's students, jumped on the project with gusto and provided valuable critiques to early drafts of the manuscript. Kim Nelson Pryor provided appreciated editing and attentive suggestions that enhanced the book considerably.

Inevitably, writing this book has taken me back to my time as an assistant professor. I am grateful for the encouragement I received during my own tenure process by my colleagues at the University of Alabama especially Claire Major and Wayne Urban. I am also profoundly grateful for the friendship and mentorship of Doug Toma, my dissertation advisor at the University of Pennsylvania. Cancer took him too early from us, but Doug influenced much of how I think about higher education. I would have loved chatting with him about this project, but even still his fingerprints are all over this book.

I am indebted to Heather Jarrow and the editorial team at Routledge. From our first meeting, Heather has been supportive of this book and made the process less stressful.

Finally, I wish to thank my family for the sacrifices they made to allow me to complete this book. My children, Rachel and Daniel, do not yet understand all this higher education stuff or why their dad has to write so much. But one day I hope they will be able to read this and understand a little bit more. My wife, Suzette, not only survived my time on the tenure-track, but now this book as well. Her positivity, encouragement, and support of our family make everything in life better.

eResources

There are eResources for this book that can be downloaded, printed, used to copy/paste text and/or manipulated to suit your individualized use. You can access these downloads by visiting the book product page on our website: www.routledge.com/9780815380931 and clicking on the eResources tab.

eRESOURCES

Part I

Learning the Rules of the Road

Chapter 1

What Is Tenure?

Tenure is a longstanding fixture in American higher education, yet it is often misunderstood both within, and outside, the academy. At a basic level, tenure is a lifetime contract that provides the protection of due process and termination only for certain causes. Within the United States, the notion of a lifetime contract with only limited causes for termination can seem foreign. Indeed, other than federal judges, it is hard to think of another industry that has something akin to tenure. Some civil servants and K-12 teachers have benefits that may provide the same, or similar, protections as tenure, but those benefits are quite different in scope (Sawchuk, 2010).

Of course, higher education's system of tenure has been criticized and debated for many years. Opponents suggest that tenure fosters laziness, disinterest in working with students, increases costs, limits institutional flexibility, and supports research of little significance (McPherson & Schapiro, 1999; McPherson & Winston, 1983). But, despite the concerns regarding tenure by administrators (Premeaux, 2008) and state legislators (McGee & Block, 2008), tenure remains an essential feature of American higher education.

Yet, the present reality for faculty has changed starkly from even a few years ago. Two out of three new hires in academia are for positions off the tenure track. In 2017, the Modern Language Association found that 67.1 percent of English faculty job advertisements were for non-tenure track positions. The number of applications for every tenure-eligible position has grown across disciplines as the number of doctorates granted increases, while the number of jobs decreases (McKenna, 2016). At the same time, the requirements and expectations for simply landing a tenure-track assistant professor position, much less tenure itself, continue to increase. There are many reasons why institutions favor non-tenure track and even part-time faculty, from financial pressure to the need for flexibility in faculty hiring (Cross & Goldenberg, 2011; Kezar, 2012). For anyone lucky enough to land a coveted tenure track professorship, the changing environment of higher education undoubtedly adds pressure to a process that was stressful under the best of circumstances (Alexander, 2000; Eagan & Garvey, 2015; Gappa, Austin, & Trice, 2007; McLendon, Hearn, & Deaton, 2006; Schuster & Finkelstein, 2006; Slaughter & Rhoades, 2004).

Given the critiques of tenure, why does the system remain in effect at most colleges and universities in the United States? The example of federal judges proves instructive. Federal judges receive lifetime appointments because we want their rulings and judgment to be based on the rule of law and not on the political winds of the moment. To help insulate judges and guard their decision making, a lifetime appointment protects them from direct or indirect societal pressure. The same argument is true for professors. Society needs scholars and teachers who seek and share knowledge free from political or societal influence; judicial decisions free from influence and based on the rule of law; and professors who are driven by knowledge, evidence, and scholarly expertise.

As a professor, I should focus on sharing my scholarly expertise when I publish my research or teach a class. If I am worried my results will offend the powers that be inside or outside the institution, I will not be able to follow the data and arguments where they lead me. Tenure, at the most basic level, protects faculty from reprisal by those who simply do not like certain areas of research or the conclusions that result. In today's hyper-partisan environment, this threat is real. In 2016, two Wisconsin legislators threatened to withhold funding from the University of Wisconsin because of a course on "The Problem of Whiteness." State Senator Dave Murphy told a local newspaper, "Is funding a course that's about 'The Problem of Whiteness' a high priority? I've got a feeling it's not" (Savidge, 2016). Given the attacks by Wisconsin Governor Scott Walker on academic freedom generally, and tenure specifically, it is clear that both opponents and supporters of tenure regularly acknowledge how influential tenure can be in guiding faculty and institutional behavior (Strauss, 2015).

The notion of protecting the creation of knowledge and the expression of ideas is at the heart of academic freedom. One of the most cited justifications for tenure is the increased protection it affords faculty. All aspects of faculty work are impacted by academic freedom including teaching, scholarship, service, and governance of the institution. In fact, in my own career, I have often found governance to be an area where academic freedom is most crucial. Whether in deciding the admission of a student from a wealthy family or disagreeing with an administrator over a policy matter, tenure gives me the protection to base my judgments on my own expertise without fearing reprisal.

Indeed, tenure has a major impact on the management, authority, and governance of higher education. While academic freedom gets much of the attention in debates over teaching and scholarship, the daily implications of tenure on the management of higher education are quite profound. In this context, tenure constrains the ability of administrators to make sweeping decisions, particularly those related to the academic mission of the university. Tenure does not give faculty absolute authority or power, but it does provide a balance against administrative decision making, or at least raises the costs of certain decisions (McPherson & Schapiro, 1999). Administrators simply cannot make decisions regarding faculty salaries, workloads, and termination without considering significant financial and political costs. These constraints on administrative authority change the behavior of both administrators and faculty. Administrators may decide the costs of a decision are not worth the price and instead focus on persuading faculty, or modifying a decision, to get faculty on board.

Tenured faculty can use their independence and voice to influence institutional decision making, which strengthens higher education (Link, Swann, & Bozeman, 2008). In addition, not only do faculty members constitute an institution's primary intellectual capital, they are also one of its few appreciable assets (Gappa & Austin, 2010). As a result, tenure plays a critical role in attracting and retaining talented faculty members by providing a high level of job security. To be sure, tenured faculty can be dismissed and are not guaranteed a job for life. However, the causes of termination are clearly outlined and create a high bar to clear, including failing to perform duties, gross misconduct, and extreme financial problems with the institution. Only employees with very strong unions have the same level of job security as tenured faculty.

As you will no doubt discover if you have not already, tenure serves as a powerful motivator for influencing faculty behavior (Link et al., 2008; Ponjuan, Conley, & Trower, 2011). During the pre-tenure years, faculty feel consistent pressure to engage in activities that will be rewarded and evaluated as part of the tenure process (Baldwin, Dezure, Shaw, & Moretto, 2008). Although elements of the tenure process can perversely incentivize and encourage faculty to engage in work they otherwise may not choose, there can be no doubt the tenure encourages faculty performance and increases productivity (Bess, 1998). Even one of the most common critiques of tenure (that the lifetime contract promotes laziness and limits productivity) implies that the process of seeking tenure actually *motivates* faculty productivity. Without a doubt, faculty work includes many privileges and flexibility that workers in many other circumstances do not enjoy. Yet, the motivation provided by tenure ensures faculty productivity in ways that can benefit both the individual and institution.

While the pursuit of tenure certainly influences faculty behavior, the decision to award tenure has a profound financial impact on a college or university. Literally, granting someone tenure commits the institution to a multimillion dollar obligation. For example, after an assistant professor is promoted and tenured, they may reasonably be expected to work for the next 35 years. With a salary of $80,300, benefits at 35%, and a 3.5% annual increase, the financial commitment by an institution is $7.2 million in current dollars (Trower, 2012). During the pre-tenure years, it can be helpful to remember the implication of tenure for the institution. Simply as good stewards of the institution, we would

5

all want our presidents and provosts to give careful consideration to the decision to spend more than $7 million worth of institutional resources. All of the hoops, stress, and requirements of the tenure process at a fundamental level are about ensuring that everyone involved in the decision to grant tenure has evaluated the tenure candidate, and also that they have thoroughly considered the fiduciary responsibility of making a sound investment.

At the same time, tenure provides a merit award for high levels of faculty productivity. This is one of the significant differences between tenure in higher education and tenure as it appears in other settings such as K-12 education. Tenure in higher education requires a level of productivity above satisfactory job performance and longevity. Regardless of whether tenure in a given situation is focused on scholarship or teaching, the tenure review process will ensure that pre-tenure faculty have achieved substantial performance and productivity to justify tenure. Thus, tenure serves as a major reward for sustained and significant merit during service as an assistant professor.

As you move along the path to tenure, remembering the various aspects of this unique career construct can provide helpful context for the process that you are undergoing. When you think about the commitment that the institution is making to you as well as the productivity that you will demonstrate during the pre-tenure years (McPherson & Winston, 1983), the overall process of going up for tenure hopefully makes a little more sense. The various stages of review; the expectations across scholarship, teaching, and service; and the required number of years of service all are justified by the rewards that stem from being granted tenure.

A BRIEF HISTORY OF TENURE

Although vestiges of the modern tenure system can be found in higher education as far back as the twelfth and thirteenth centuries, tenure as we know it today is largely a by-product of the twentieth century. Aspects of today's tenure system—such as faculty rank, longer lifetime appointments, and evaluation for performance—appeared in fits and starts during the 1800s. After the Civil War, colleges and universities began adopting the German higher education model, which emphasized science and research to an extent atypical even among the best American colleges of the day. With the growth of this research university model, American professors began to expect the same perks that their German colleagues enjoyed, including indefinite appointments except in cases of gross dereliction of duty (Hofstadter & Metzger, 1955). In many ways, the tenure system can be directly tied back to the founding of the American Association of University Professors (AAUP) in 1915. Founders, including noted education philosopher John Dewey, sought protections for faculty after a series of highly publicized cases in which prominent faculty members were dismissed because of unpopular views. Considered alongside a rise in disciplinary associations, the times demanded a strong voice supporting the role of faculty in higher education. The AAUP was formed as an organization that would advocate across all disciplines and higher education institutions.

With its founding, the AAUP promoted the value of academic freedom and, ultimately, the necessity of the "security of tenure" to protect this important ideal. The AAUP put forth the first forceful case for the necessity of tenure in supporting the teaching and research missions of higher education. Yet, the concept of tenure was still relatively in flux until a more definitive statement on tenure was put forward in 1940. At this time, the *Statement of Principles on Academic Freedom and Tenure* was jointly created by the AAUP and the Association of American Colleges and Universities and remains the most significant document related to tenure in the history of the United States. In fact, you may find reference in your institution's tenure policies to upholding the principles outlined in this statement. The *Statement of Principles on Academic Freedom and Tenure* provided a clear and stable concept of tenure, which remains the guiding framework across higher education today.

A key element of the AAUP's original 1915 statement was the inclusion of judicial proceedings and due process as part of tenure. In addition, the AAUP established the guiding principle of a probationary period recognizable as the pre-tenure years. The idea was that assistant professors would need to successfully complete a probationary period before receiving tenure (Pollitt & Kurland, 1998). You will certainly recognize the due process elements and the requirement of a probationary period as part of the tenure process that today's pre-tenure faculty undergo.

The AAUP's 1940 Statement identifies the purposes of tenure as follows:

(1) freedom of teaching and research and of extramural activities, and (2) a sufficient degree of economic security to make the profession attractive to men and women of ability. Freedom and economic security, hence, tenure, are indispensable to the success of an institution in fulfilling its obligations to its students and to society.

In addition, the AAUP stated that faculty dismissal should be determined by a faculty trial, with written charges, and only for adequate cause. The clear purpose of these policies would be to protect professors by offering rights of due process and access to a jury of their colleagues. From the very beginning, there was a legal element of the tenure process that remains an important aspect today. Finally, while affirming that untenured faculty had the same rights to academic freedom as their tenured colleagues, the AAUP statement importantly clarified the probationary review process. The process was tied to years of service and specified that the pre-tenure period should not exceed seven years, which remains a component of most tenure policies.

As you learn more about your own institution's tenure policies, it can be helpful to understand the historical legacies that still profoundly influence the framework of tenure and promotion. One of the reasons tenure processes and policies bear remarkable similarities across institutions is that, while higher education institutions have existed for centuries, tenure was created over the past 100 years, making it a relatively new concept. The importance of faculty evaluation along with administrative review is born out of the initial rationale for creating tenure. The basic steps that assistant professors will follow while going up for tenure are largely the same ones outlined by the AAUP back in 1940. Tenure policies and procedures were designed from the beginning to promote the mission of higher education and not to provide leverage to either the faculty member or the institution. Furthermore, the AAUP's goal, which by most standards was quite successful, was to promote common procedures for tenure. As I will discuss throughout this book, the emphasis and evaluation criteria may differ between institutions—but the process is substantively similar. This benefits assistant professors by enabling them to focus on their pre-tenure work without having to learn an idiosyncratic process that may be quite different from institution to institution. As a result, pre-tenure faculty and institutions have a relatively well-established process and procedure for evaluating faculty at the conclusion of the probationary period.

PAUSE AND REFLECT

Take a moment to review your institution's policies for tenure and promotion. Identify the key criteria for tenure and any aspects of the policies that seem unclear to you. Use the space provided below to outline the expectations and your unanswered questions.

Key criteria for tenure:

_____

_____

Areas needing clarity:

_____

_____

Expectations and questions:

_____

_____

TENURE PROCESS(ES)

While we often refer to the tenure process as if it is a single process that assistant professors undergo, the reality is the tenure process constitutes three interrelated streams that work both together and at cross purposes. The tenure process is comprised of a legal process, a peer review process, and a political process.

Legal Process

Since the AAUP's original statements related to tenure called for due process and legal protections for faculty, the tenure process has always contained a significant element of legality. While undergoing the process for tenure, pre-tenure faculty must always remember that this legal aspect will create the same degree of formality and due process that you would expect in any other legal proceeding. Policies and procedures as well as court cases and legal precedent guide decisions regarding tenure, and the dossier and other written documentation required during the process are critically important precisely because of the legal nature of tenure.

While we often think of tenure as simply an institutional evaluation of the teaching, research, and service activities of a faculty member, its legal implications are quite real. Tenure establishes, for example, the legal causes for which faculty may be terminated. Its guidelines create property rights and contract law implications as well as due process criteria. As a result, no matter the academic discipline or institution, the tenure process includes legal elements that must be considered by the candidate as well as the institution. This legality protects both parties, increases the necessity of formality, and provides remedies for faculty who believe they have been treated inappropriately or unfairly.

Peer Review Process

Beyond the legal process involved in tenure, faculty are likely more familiar with the peer-review (GLOBAL) process that occurs throughout the tenure review. Similar to the process by which academic publications are peer reviewed as part of publication, in the tenure process the overall case for tenure is reviewed by academic peers in the department, school, institution, and discipline. Through the use of external reviewers (discussed in more detail in Chapter 6), the peer review process brings an element of disciplinary peer-review into the tenure process. Throughout the various stages of tenure case review within the institution, peers evaluate whether pre-tenure faculty have met the criteria laid out for them under institutional policies and guidelines for promotion and tenure.

For those outside of higher education and not accustomed to peer review, this process can seem unusual, if not downright bizarre; in essence, colleagues have a direct say in whether or not you keep your job. At times, this can even be

9

disorienting: One moment you and your colleagues share equal voice and vote on departmental issues, while the next your entire professional career is laid out for judgment by these same peers. Just as we in American society value a jury by one's peers in, for example, the criminal justice system, faculty value that colleagues, with scholarly expertise and experience, make judgments regarding the suitability of someone for tenure. This does not mean, however, that the process is without challenges. While administrators certainly have a voice in the process, faculty colleagues have a direct and early influence upon the outcome of a tenure case. Peer review, thus, is vital to the tenure process and proves one of the most influential elements in determining a final decision.

Political Process

In addition to the legal and peer-review processes at play, tenure involves a political process that can create perhaps the most uncertainty and ambiguity throughout the process. The political process as part of tenure includes interactions and negotiations between various groups (i.e. pre-tenure faculty, tenured faculty, and administrators) as well as balancing different goals, values, and interests. For better or worse, a tenure case is not simply decided on the merits of a candidate–it is also influenced by politics. The political process may work for or against you, but it can undoubtedly make the tenure process more complicated, especially for those not used to navigating within this context. Certainly, being a wunderkind with institutional politics does not replace a strong teaching and research record as evidenced by the dossier, but candidates also cannot ignore the political reality of tenure.

Once pre-tenure faculty start to realize the inherent political process at work with tenure, it becomes reasonable to devise an approach to successfully navigate these waters. Whicker, Kronenfeld, and Strickland (1993) compared the tenure process to a political legislative process. Legislatures have rules and traditions that guide their work, but they can also be freewheeling, swayed by powerful interests and public perception. Powerful constituents, both formal and informal, may play a significant role in the final decision. While at times you may wish that the tenure process was an apolitical meritocracy, you will nevertheless need to navigate the political process in order to provide a foundation for your tenure case to be considered on its merits.

MANAGING YOUR IMAGE

Given the political nature of tenure, as a pre-tenure faculty member you must keep in mind how to manage your professional image. Throughout the tenure process, you will need a strategy to manage your professional image in order to help keep the focus on your accomplishments and competence for your work.

PAUSE AND REFLECT

Take a moment to reflect on how others perceive you and your work. If you asked your colleagues to describe your qualities, characteristics, and overall impression of you as a faculty member, what would they say?

_____

_____

_____

_____

Roberts (2005) described professional image as the qualities and characteristics that influence how others perceive your professional competence and character.

Did this exercise make you uncomfortable? Did you initially think that you were going to do your work and let others think what they will? If you answered yes to these questions, it is quite possible that managing your image will be something you struggle with and have to focus on during your pre-tenure years. Professional image can be important in communicating with others and sharing your accomplishments. Even tenured colleagues who know you well and are familiar with your work will likely not fully understand all you do as a faculty member. Everyone is busy and focused on his or her own activities. Thus, it is important that pre-tenure faculty cultivate a professional image of competence in doing important and significant scholarly work.

Many faculty struggle from either doing too much or too little self-promoting. If you are perceived as bragging about your accomplishments or overblowing the significance of your work, your colleagues may hold a negative impression of you. Conversely, you cannot assume that people know what you are working on and have achieved in the past. You will have to communicate with your dean, department chair, and colleagues in order for them to appreciate all you are doing during the pre-tenure years. Although there are pre-tenure faculty who certainly go overboard with self-promotion (and I suspect we could all name a few because of the negative impression they foster), I would argue that _most_ pre-tenure faculty instead struggle to sufficiently promote their work. Unfortunately, it is simply not enough to work hard and succeed academically if no one knows about it. This may mean that you need to share journal acceptances with your department chair or copies of your work with colleagues at other institutions. Promoting your work also means you will need to travel to conferences and other institutions or deliver lectures on your research, for example, in order to familiarize people with your work.

11

In the age of social media, you must also actively manage your professional online identity. In fact, if you are at an institution with limited resources, particularly for conference travel, social media can be a useful approach to increase your reputation so long as you keep the management of social media in check with your other responsibilities. When someone types your name into Google, I am sure you would prefer they find your professional website rather than a news story of the serial killer who shares your name. Effectively managing your online image includes *actively* updating and maintaining a professional website. Some faculty use their institution's faculty page, while others create websites of their own. While you must consider how much time, money, and effort are involved in managing your web presence, your primary goal is to cultivate a professional image that will support your tenure case (Georgina & Olson, 2008). If you decide to create your own website you should include, at minimum, "About Me," "CV," and "Contact Information" pages. Whether you create your own site or use your institutional page, the most important thing is to ensure these pages are regularly updated. You do not need to update them for every single new publication, but you do not want them to be years out of date, either. To manage this for myself, I set a calendar alert to remind me on January 1 and July 1 to update my institutional webpage. During my pre-tenure years I did this more frequently, approximately every three months.

Social media can also have profound implications for your professional image (Gruzd, Staves, & Wilk, 2011; Gruzd, Staves, & Wilk, 2012). In the near future, assistant professors who grew up using social media will enter the faculty ranks; this may cause challenges regarding social media to grow and change. For now, however, the usual advice one hears about social media—be careful about photographs, privacy settings, and online posts—are as true for pre-tenure faculty as they are for any individual taking part in a job search. In particular, you should never discuss students online. Even if you have strict privacy settings, it is possible that what you post will get out and back to the students. There are numerous cases of professors who have posted on Facebook about a class, perhaps disparaging the quality of the students. Somehow, students end up acquiring a screenshot of the post. I am sure you can imagine the comments on the course evaluations at the end of those classes. Do yourself a favor—do not discuss students on social media.

Given the political nature of the tenure process, others' perceptions of your work will have a significant impact on your tenure case. To be sure, your professional image, even a positive one, is no replacement for actual accomplishments. Moreover, we have to acknowledge that tenure review committees may review candidates with similar accomplishments differently. From various biases to impressions of someone's work, the tenure process includes subjective elements that belies completely objective judgements. Whether you are an avid Twitter user or someone uncomfortable with self-promotion, a strong professional identity helps you put your best foot forward in the tenure process. Just as you craft your research agenda and build connections with scholars in your field, you will need to shape your professional identity and strategically influence how those at your institution view you and the quality of your work. This work is critical to the well-being of your tenure case, and to you as a professional.

Understanding Culture, Norms, and Socialization

One of the biggest challenges in writing a book like this is the impossibility of fully capturing the variety that exists across higher education. As the noted anthropologist Clifford Geertz (1994) suggested, culture shapes, and is shaped by, the social interactions of people in the organization. At a practical level, this means that tenure can vary across departments and schools within one institution, to say nothing of the differences to be found when looking across institutions. While there are similarities in terms of policies and procedures, the particulars of culture can influence the reality of tenure. In this section, I want to discuss faculty socialization, culture, and norms. My purpose, for those unfamiliar with these concepts, is to help you to be a better observer of your own circumstances. Throughout this book, I note where differences exist across higher education, but only you will be able to determine what is most appropriate in your individual circumstances. My hope is that you are able to take the following suggestions into account to help you determine the best approach for successfully navigating tenure.

Faculty Socialization

Faculty culture builds from the collective socialization experiences that influence faculty values, beliefs, and attitudes, and it occurs in two primary stages. First, *anticipatory socialization* includes your graduate education, during which you are exposed to the culture and norms of higher education and your discipline. Second, *organizational socialization* begins after you are hired as a new assistant professor (Austin, 2002). By muddling through a trial and error process (Van Maanen & Schein, 1979), you face organizational challenges and find ways to manage the realities of academic work. Much of the frustration, loneliness, time pressure, and workload facing pre-tenure faculty evolves from the process of organizational socialization as you move from a novice to an experienced member of the organization.

As a cultural process, tenure serves as a rite of passage to status in the institution (Tierney & Bensimon, 1996; Tierney & Rhoads, 1994). While socialization remains ongoing throughout the faculty career, the initial learning process

13

proves influential and demanding during the first few years on the tenure track. Additionally, socialization is not a one-way street. As you inevitability adapt to your new institution and department, it also adapts to you. As I note throughout this book, you will, at times, adjust your priorities to those valued as part of tenure at your institution. Likewise, your institution will also undergo a review of tenure in light of you and your other pre-tenure colleagues. The bidirectional nature of socialization means that the expectations and process of tenure is continually reviewed and refined.

Culture and Norms of Your Institution

Tierney and Rhoads (1994) identify the various levels of faculty culture that exist in higher education. The table below identifies the primary levels that influence faculty work.

Specific to the tenure process, the levels of disciplinary and institutional culture are quite significant. Assuming that you received substantial disciplinary socialization as part of your doctoral experience, I focus my discussion here on institutional culture.

Faculty culture operates within the broader organizational culture of the institution. The influences of culture from the national, disciplinary, or individual level also occur within the context of your college or university. The culture of the institution derives from how the college communicates its mission and the meaning behind it, as well as how members of the campus community interpret the mission (Eckel, 2008; Hartley, 2002; Morphew & Hartley, 2006). Of course, various well-known institutional attributes mediate how this communication and interpretation occurs, including an institution's size, public versus private control, religious orientation, and other factors (Harris, 2013). The mission, leadership,

TABLE 1.1 Faculty Cultures

Faculty Culture Level	Characteristic
National culture	Varies by country & society
Professional culture	Varies by occupation
Disciplinary culture	Varies by area of study
Institutional culture	Varies by institution (type, size, location, private vs. public, etc.)
Individual cultural differences	Varies by personal quality

(Tierney & Rhoads, 1994)

values, and symbols that give your institution its identity also influence the daily work of faculty before, during, and after tenure (Platter, 1995).

As a pre-tenure faculty member, one of your challenges occurs when cultures conflict with one another. In fact, one of the most effective ways to identify culture is when it conflicts or overlaps with another. Faculty members are on the front lines of negotiating these conflicts and attempting to come to a resolution, while at the same time retaining to some degree, the values and beliefs of the institution, school, department, and their colleagues. Sometimes, these challenges may be solved by a simple compromise, while others may lead you to a different institution.

One of the most common examples of how levels of faculty culture can conflict in light of tenure are concepts referred to in the literature as *cosmopolitan* and *local faculty* (Baker & Zey-Ferrell, 1984; Berger & Grimes, 1973; Fuller, Hester, Barnett, & Relyea, 2006). "Cosmopolitan" faculty have low levels of loyalty to their home institution and have high levels of commitment to their discipline, holding values and beliefs tied to their disciplines even if these are not shared at their institution. "Local faculty," in contrast, have great loyalty to and affinity with their campus and relatively lower levels of commitment to the discipline. Frequently, this juxtaposition arises where faculty receive their graduate training compared to where they establish their faculty careers. Most faculty are trained in research universities and receive socialization into that culture. Yet, many faculty are employed in institutions where research is not the primary mission. Despite the different mission of their new institutions, recently hired assistant professors often seek to bring the culture and norms of their graduate institutions to their new academic homes (Austin, 2002). This mismatch can create conflict and cause problems in the tenure process for pre-tenure faculty.

The Ritual of Tenure

If socialization and culture provide the context for faculty work, the tenure and promotion process serves as the ritual rite of passage for new faculty. While everyone understands the outcome of a ritual such as tenure (you are either granted tenure or not), the ritual's process is more opaque. Upon arriving on campus, pre-tenure faculty begin receiving information, feedback, and cultural cues regarding the tenure ritual of that institution. Pre-tenure faculty may receive contradictory advice or guidance—not as a result of malicious intent, but because the process is opaque even to those institutional actors involved in the decision-making process. The tenure ritual, then, is embedded within the broader culture of the institution and the discipline. Thus, tenure rituals can prove beneficial to organizations as the process allows new or novice members to move into a place of higher status and experience.

15

Cultural Analysis

Given the notions of socialization, culture, and ritual described here, how should pre-tenure faculty attempt to analyze and identify these elements at their own institution? Some analysis can, and ideally should, be done during the job search process, but other elements can only be fully understood once you have become a member of the community. Edgar Schein (2010), a prominent scholar of organizational studies, developed a framework for analyzing an organization's culture that may prove useful to assistant professors as you begin to understand the culture of your new institution. His model refers to three levels of culture: artifacts, espoused values, and assumption. Schein's seminal work suggests that an observer can identify specific cultural markers and phenomena that foster understanding of the culture of an organization.

Artifacts constitute the most superficial level of culture and include tangible elements that can be identified by individuals outside the organization. Dress codes, imagery, slogans, and commonly used terminology may be considered artifacts. Next, espoused values encompass the stated values and behaviors identified as foundational by organizational members. These value statements shared by both the organization and its individual members describe the key priorities of the organization. Mission statements, vision statements, tenure policies, annual reports, and speeches may all be examples of espoused values. As you can tell from these examples, both artifacts and espoused values may be at least partially identified by an outsider. If you did not identify these during your job search process, you should begin to do so as quickly as possible, ideally before you arrive on campus.

The final level of culture in Schein's work are underlying assumptions. This level captures the deeply held, possibly unstated beliefs maintained by the organization. Often, this level of culture is difficult to fully capture and articulate even among members of the organization, since these are often unspoken or unwritten beliefs. An often-cited analogy, for example, is how would a fish describe water? It exists at such a fundamental level that a fish cannot imagine life without it. The underlying assumption here proves the same for organizations, whose members can be so well integrated and ingrained in their culture that it can be hard for them to recognize or articulate their cultural beliefs. While you may have picked up on some elements of these during the campus visit as part of your job search, you likely will be unable to fully identify these until you arrive on campus.

According to Schein (2010), at times, the only way you may be able to identify an underlying assumption is when you do something to violate the norms it has established. Cultures and ritual processes pressure organizational members, pre-tenure faculty in this case, to either conform or leave the institution. Violating a norm built on an underlying assumption may not be fatal to a tenure case, yet repeated violations will likely prove detrimental. The ritual of tenure provides an institutional mechanism to encourage conformity and compliance, so much so that critics of tenure may consider this tendency a negative aspect of the process that overemphasizes compliance and exacerbates homogeneity.

As a new assistant professor on campus, you should keenly observe your campus culture, including the culture of your school and department. When you meet people, attend events, and have discussions with colleagues, keep an eye out for elements of culture that can help you identify the values and beliefs of your institution. Your tenure process will be influenced by these cultural components; thus, the sooner you can identify them, the better to contextualize your unique process (which will differ in large and small ways from colleagues across campus or across the country). By developing this cultural awareness, you will be in a position to apply the advice provided later in this book. I have noted differences where they are obvious, but in various ways your individual circumstances will require adjustments from what I have outlined here. A cultural analysis along the lines of what I have discussed in this section will provide a critical vantage point from which you can adjust the advice and tenure strategies you read here and receive from mentors, senior colleagues, and others during your pre-tenure years.

PAUSE AND REFLECT

Take a moment to identify the elements of your institution's culture and norms around faculty work using Schein's levels of culture.

Artifacts:

_____

_____

Espoused values:

_____

_____

Assumptions:

_____

_____

Considering all 3 levels, describe your institution's culture in a sentence or two:

_____

_____

FACULTY LOAD

When considering the expectations for tenure, one of the key variables in the mix is the typical teaching load for your institution. Your teaching load will have a direct impact on the other expectations of the tenure process. In discussing teaching loads, you will often hear answers such as, "I teach a 1–2," or, "I teach a 4–4." Faculty teaching loads for full-time, tenure eligible faculty are described using X–Y phrasing, where X equals the number of courses you regularly teach in the fall while Y equals the number of courses you teach in the spring. For example, "I teach a 1–2" means that you teach one course in the fall and two in the spring. Most full-time faculty contracts are for the 9-month academic year, thus we typically refer to the fall and spring semesters. In unusual cases, a summer class or class taught during a short term (i.e., January term) may count for load, but these are typically considered above the normal load and you might receive extra compensation for teaching them. Faculty loads are often the same across fall and spring semesters, although you will certainly find examples where the load varies. In the examples below describing how teaching load may impact the other expectations of tenure, I use an equal load across semesters. However, if your load is different you can adjust the expectations up or down accordingly.

4–4

For a faculty member on a 4–4 load, there are rarely formal expectations regarding research, and it is even possible that you will see lower expectations for service responsibilities as well. A 4–4 teaching load is typically the highest teaching load you will find in a four-year college or university. Community college faculty may teach a 5–5 load, but if you are in a four-year institution, teaching 3-credit hour classes, then four courses per term is about the highest teaching load you will find. A 4–4 load usually means that you are on an exclusively teaching assignment, as is most often the case for instructors, lecturers, professors of practice, and other non-tenure eligible faculty positions.

3–3

Faculty employed at small private colleges and regional comprehensive universities will often teach a 3–3 load. As a result, the expectations for research productivity tend to be lower. For example, while some evidence of scholarly publication may be expected for earning tenure, the primary focus will be on teaching. Unlike faculty on a 4–4 load, faculty with a 3–3 will often have significant service responsibilities. If you are at a striving university (Gonzales, Martinez, & Ordu, 2014), your expectations could be even more demanding. Striving institutions are those that have historically focused more on teaching, but seek to become stronger research universities. On such a campus, faculty will often retain a 3–3 teaching load and experience high service demands, *but also* have greater research expectations. Faculty in striving universities face significant pressures to meet research expectations comparable to those at research universities, yet also continue meeting the long-standing demands of teaching universities (Gardner & Veliz, 2014; Gonzales et al., 2014).

2–2

At research universities, tenure track faculty most frequently teach a 2–2 load. Whether the courses are undergraduate or graduate level, they often count the same in terms of the teaching load. For tenure, faculty on a 2–2 load are expected to have a high level of research activity in addition to significant levels of institutional and professional service. When we commonly discuss tenure in higher education, an assistant professor serving at a research university on a 2–2 is stereotypical. On a 2–2 load, pre-tenure faculty have a mix of teaching, research, and service obligations that must be met in order to meet the expectations for tenure.

Less than a 2–2

While at most research universities you will find a 2–2 load, you may witness situations in which a pre-tenure faculty member teaches fewer than two courses per semester. While it is possible the university may have a lower teaching expectation, it is more likely a faculty member will be released from teaching a course because of grant activity or administrative work. If you have heard of a faculty member who is "bought out of teaching," for instance, this means that a grant pays the part of their salary that would have been paid for by teaching a class. This enables the faculty member to spend more time on the grant project and on their scholarship. Although unusual for pre-tenure faculty, some faculty receive teaching releases for administrative work. As an example, department chairs frequently have a lower teaching load to compensate for the time they spend on administrative duties.

PROBATIONARY PERIOD

Thanks to the widespread adoption of the principles laid out by the AAUP statement on tenure (Euben, 2002), most higher education institutions follow a relatively similar process regarding the time pre-tenure faculty will spend prior to going up for tenure, also called the probationary period. Generally, assistant professors will spend no more than seven years on the tenure clock, at which time a decision will be made regarding tenure. This decision is colloquially called "up or out" or simply "going up" for tenure. Since the tenure review process typically takes as much as a year, it will often begin at the beginning of the sixth year in order to yield a final decision by the start of the seventh year.

The seven-year timeframe was established to provide sufficient time for pre-tenure faculty to demonstrate their productivity and ability without proving so long as to be unsustainable. Generally, in the contract letter appointing an assistant professor a member of the faculty, a date will be included by which a decision will be made regarding tenure. Most commonly, the time on the tenure clock starts as soon as you become an assistant professor at the institution. Few institutions will give credit for time spent prior to receiving a doctorate or during years served as a postdoc researcher. The idea is that a professor will spend six years as a pre-tenure faculty member before the tenure decision is made.

If you are just beginning as a new, pre-tenure faculty member, six or seven years can seem like an awfully long time to keep the pace necessary to successfully receive tenure. Admittedly, six years is a long time and can be frustrating and draining. However, when you think about the institutional investment noted earlier, six years of productivity with the return of 30 or 40 years of permanent employment appears a little more reasonable. Moreover, given the realities of academic publishing, the time before tenure is more compressed than even six years.

A common question regarding the tenure clock is what happens when a pre-tenure faculty member moves institutions during the probationary period. There are typically two outcomes, determined largely by the views of the dean at the new institution. The first is that the new hire negotiates time credit served at another institution as part of their new tenure contract. For example, if you served two years as an assistant professor at Institution A, then you may negotiate for Institution B to let you start in your third year on the tenure track there. The second is that the new hire starts the tenure clock over at the new institution. Some deans have a philosophical belief that you should spend the full tenure clock at their institution. This point is negotiated during the search process so that the contract can indicate when you need to go up for tenure.

Even if your hiring dean is amenable to bringing in time from another institution, there are a few reasons why you may not want to do this. The most common reason may be that your productivity was insufficient during the years in question and you would be better off starting over. Another common reason may be that the tenure expectations at the new institution are quite different from the previous one and you need to spend your time differently. Finally, even if the new dean agrees to let you bring in time, it is common that you will be expected to serve at least one year prior to being considered for tenure. This is often true if you have not received tenure at your previous institution; the new institution will want to take you out for a test drive, so to speak, and ensure that you meet their expectations as a faculty member and colleague prior to granting tenure. As a final note, there are always exceptions granted for various reasons, so you may find that your particular situation differs from those described here.

Pausing the Tenure Clock

Once the tenure clock starts, it is not typical to stop it. A decision to pause the tenure clock is guided by the policies and procedures of the institution. But, regardless of the reason for a pause, any stoppage will typically last at least one year. Because of the amount of time that it takes to conduct a tenure review, it simply is not possible to handle off-cycle reviews. So, while you may only want to pause your clock for a month or two, in the vast majority of cases you will be required to either stay on time or delay for at least a year. The most common reason that pre-tenure faculty pause their tenure clock is due to a major change in life circumstances such as medical or parental leave (Manchester, Leslie, & Kramer, 2013). Institutions have progressed somewhat in offering leave as part of supporting work-life balance among faculty; nevertheless, these policies can vary substantially and you should investigate what your institution offers to new parents or caregivers (Thornton, 2005; Ward & Wolf-Wendel, 2004).

Whether you are considering pausing your tenure clock due to a new child or a medical issue, you should take into account the politics involved in a decision to pause the clock. If the institution has a policy, for example, of granting a one-year pause for new parents, then you absolutely have the right to avail yourself of it. Unfortunately, however, such a decision may not be straightforward. If there are faculty in your department who decided not to take a leave, might taking one put you at a disadvantage? In other circumstances, leave can even prove advantageous. I knew a colleague once who decided to take a family leave, at least in part, to allow more time to get manuscripts published. Leave for this reason is quite problematic and takes advantage of a policy, which can cause problems for your case, as well as for those of other pre-tenure colleagues who may legitimately seek to take a leave.

All this to say, issues regarding the decision to stop the tenure clock can prove more complicated than they may first appear. Prior to making any decisions regarding the tenure clock, I strongly suggest you discuss questions or concerns and try to get a sense of the institutional and departmental norms from the dean, department chair, senior colleagues, and mentors. I want to reiterate that everyone should feel permitted to take advantage of the policies that the institution provides to support faculty's professional and personal lives. However, I also want you to be fully informed, and understand the nuances that may be involved, including those which may not appear on the surface, before making a decision. At the end of the day, the tenure clock exists to protect both pre-tenure faculty and the institution, and I advise you to consider all the possibilities before making any decisions altering the tenure clock.

21

INTERIM CONTRACTS

Related to the idea of the tenure clock, pre-tenure faculty may receive shorter-term contracts prior to the institution's decision regarding tenure. These contracts may vary, depending on institution, from a series of one-year contracts to two medium-term contracts (i.e., two three-year contracts). Although there may be technical provisions that allow a dean to not renew a contract because of poor performance, generally speaking these contracts automatically renew at their conclusion. The most significant exception to this rule is the conclusion of the mid-tenure review. Typically, and occurring during the third or fourth year on the tenure track, the mid-tenure review allows colleagues and decision-makers to comprehensively review the current state of the tenure case, provide critique and feedback of activities thus far, and make a preliminary decision regarding the likelihood of an assistant professor successfully receiving tenure.

If those reviewing the case at the mid-tenure review believe that a faculty member has zero chance of receiving tenure for whatever reason, he or she may be counseled to consider other opportunities or, most dramatically, may not have their contract renewed. However, the mid-tenure review is not designed to replace the "up or out" decision that comes at the end of the probationary period. It is obviously more humane and collegial to let someone know if their tenure chances are remote, as well as to provide an appropriate process for providing substantial review. Except in the most egregious cases, pre-tenure faculty continue to have opportunities to build the case for tenure and to be considered at the end of the tenure clock.

BE A SCHOLAR OF THE TENURE PROCESS

During graduate school, students are well-trained in the theories, methods, and research approaches in their disciplines. While there may have been some professional seminars that provided information and socialization regarding tenure, I would guess that very few assistant professors have received significant exposure to how to successfully navigate the tenure and promotion process. At best, faculty understand research and teaching, but have little exposure to all the elements involved in getting tenure.

My goal with this book is to help you become a scholar of the tenure process. I encourage you to approach tenure in similar ways as you would address problems in your field. Obviously, your first focus will be on your primary research, teaching, and service work, but your tenure case will also benefit from an intellectual curiosity regarding how tenure works. It is worth some investment in time and energy to understand the background of tenure, the key components and considerations, and how the process works at your institution. If your institution or discipline offers workshops for pre-tenure faculty, attend as many of these as possible. Schedule meetings with mentors and senior colleagues to seek their advice and counsel regarding tenure. Additionally, identify and regularly discuss your tenure case with the tenured faculty in your department.

One of the challenges in learning about the tenure process is that pre-tenure faculty will often receive contradictory, or even completely wrong, information or advice. You still need to communicate with senior faculty in the department and school, even if you cannot take all the advice at face value. Reading books such as this one, reading *The Chronicle of Higher Education* and *InsideHigherEd.com*, and seeking other sources of information about tenure can provide a framework to understand and excel in your pursuit of tenure. As with any research question you may have, making use of the research literature and multiple sources of data and evidence will improve your knowledge and answer your questions. Becoming a scholar of tenure will help you navigate the challenges that come with the process and ensure that you are doing all you can to receive a letter at the end of the tenure probationary period that says, "Congratulations, you will receive tenure and be promoted to the rank of associate professor."

REFERENCES

Alexander, F. K. (2000). The changing face of accountability: Monitoring and assessing institutional performance in higher education. *The Journal of Higher Education*, *71*(4), 411–431.

Austin, A. E. (2002). Preparing the next generation of faculty: Graduate school as socialization to the academic career. *Journal of Higher Education*, *73*(1), 94–112.

Baker, P. J., & Zey-Ferrell, M. (1984). Local and cosmopolitan orientations of faculty: Implications for teaching. *Teaching Sociology*, *12*(1), 82–106.

Baldwin, R., Dezure, D., Shaw, A., & Moretto, K. (2008). Mapping the terrain of mid-career faculty at a research university: Implications for faculty and academic leaders. *Change: The Magazine of Higher Learning*, *40*(5), 46–55.

Berger, P. K., & Grimes, A. (1973). Cosmopolitan-local: A factor analysis of the construct. *Administrative Science Quarterly*, *18*(2), 223–235.

Bess, J. L. (1998). Contract systems, bureaucracies, and faculty motivation: The probable effects of a no-tenure policy. *The Journal of Higher Education*, *69*(1), 1–22.

Cross, J. G., & Goldenberg, E. N. (2011). *Off-track profs: Nontenured teachers in higher education*. Cambridge, MA: MIT Press.

Eagan, K. J., & Garvey, J. C. (2015). Stressing out: Connecting race, gender, and stress with faculty productivity. *The Journal of Higher Education*, *86*(6), 923–954.

Eckel, P. D. (2008). Mission diversity and the tension between prestige and effectiveness: An overview of US higher education. *Higher Education Policy*, *21*(2), 175–192.

Euben, D. R. (2002). Tenure: Perspectives and challenges. Retrieved from www.aaup.org/issues/tenure/tenure-perspectives-and-challenges-2002.

Fuller, B. J., Hester, K., Barnett, T., & Relyea, L. (2006). Perceived organizational support and perceived external prestige: Predicting organizational attachment for university faculty, staff, and administrators. *Journal of Social Psychology*, *146*(3), 327–347.

Gappa, J. M., & Austin, A. E. (2010). Rethinking academic traditions for twenty-first century faculty. *AAUP Journal of Academic Freedom*, *1*(1), 1–20.

Gappa, J. M., Austin, A. F., & Trice, A. G. (2007). *Rethinking faculty work: Higher education's strategic imperative*. San Francisco, CA: Jossey-Bass.

Gardner, S. K., & Veliz, D. (2014). Evincing the ratchet: A thematic analysis of the promotion and tenure guidelines at a striving university. *Review of Higher Education*, *38*(1), 105–132.

Geertz, C. (1994). Thick description: Toward an interpretive theory of culture. In M. Martin & L. McIntyre (Eds.), *Readings in The Philosophy of Social Science*. Cambridge, MA: MIT Press.

Georgina, D. A., & Olson, M. R. (2008). Integration of technology in higher education: A review of faculty self-perceptions. *The Internet and Higher Education*, *11*(1), 1–8.

Gonzales, L. D., Martinez, E., & Ordu, C. (2014). Exploring faculty experiences in a striving university through the lens of academic capitalism. *Studies in Higher Education*, *39*(7), 1097–1115.

Gruzd, A., Staves, K., & Wilk, A. (2011). Tenure and promotion in the age of online social media. *Proceedings of the American Society for Information Science and Technology*, *48*(1), 1–9.

Gruzd, A., Staves, K., & Wilk, A. (2012). Connected scholars: Examining the role of social media in research practices of faculty using the UTAUT model. *Computers in Human Behavior*, *28*(6), 2340–2350.

Harris, M. S. (2013). *Understanding institutional diversity in American higher education*. San Francisco, CA: Jossey-Bass.

Hartley, M. (2002). *A call to purpose: Mission-centered change in three liberal arts colleges*. New York, NY: Routledge.

Hofstadter, R., & Metzger, N. (1955). *The development of academic freedom in the United States*. New York, NY: Columbia University Press.

Kezar, A. J. (Ed.) (2012). *Embracing non-tenure track faculty: Changing campuses for the new faculty majority*. New York, NY: Routledge.

Link, A. N., Swann, C. A., & Bozeman, B. (2008). A time allocation study of university faculty. *Economics of Education Review*, *27*(4), 363–374.

McGee, R. W., & Block, W. E. (2008). Academic tenure: An economic critique. In W. Block (Ed.), *Labor Economics from a Free Market Perspective*. Singapore: World Scientific.

McKenna, L. (2016, April 21). The ever-tightening job market for Ph.D.s: Why do so many people continue to pursue doctorates? *The Atlantic*. Retrieved from www.theatlantic.com/education/archive/2016/04/bad-job-market-phds/479205/

McLendon, M. K., Hearn, J. C., & Deaton, R. (2006). Called to account: Analyzing the origins and spread of state performance accountability policies for higher education. *Educational Evaluation and Policy Analysis*, *28*(1), 1–24.

McPherson, M. S., & Schapiro, M. O. (1999). Tenure issues in higher education. *The Journal of Economic Perspectives*, *13*(1), 85–98.

McPherson, M. S., & Winston, G. C. (1983). The economics of academic tenure: A relational perspective. *Journal of Economic Behavior and Organization*, *4*(2–3), 163–184.

Manchester, C. F., Leslie, L. M., & Kramer, A. (2013). Is the clock still ticking? An evaluation of the consequences of stopping the tenure clock. *IRL Review*, *66*(1), 3–31.

Modern Language Association. (2017). Report on the MLA job information list, 2015–16. Retrieved from www.mla.org/content/download/58256/1846498/RptJIL15_16.pdf

Morphew, C. C., & Hartley, M. (2006). Mission statements: A thematic analysis of rhetoric across institutional type. *Journal of Higher Education*, *77*(3), 456–471.

Platter, W. M. (1995). Future work faculty time in the 21st century. *Change: The Magazine of Higher Learning*, *27*(3), 22–33.

Pollitt, D. H., & Kurland, J. E. (1998). Entering the academic freedom arena running: The AAUP's first year. *Academe*, *84*(4), 45–52.

Ponjuan, L., Conley, V. M., & Trower, C. A. (2011). Career stage differences in pre-tenure track faculty perceptions of professional and personal relationships with colleagues. *The Journal of Higher Education*, *82*(3), 319–346.

Premeaux, S. R. (2008). Adminstrative versus faculty perspectives regarding academic tenure. *The Journal of Academic Administration in Higher Education*, *4*(1), 47–55.

Roberts, L. M. (2005). Changing faces: Professional image construction in diverse organizational settings. *Academy of Management Review*, *30*(4), 685–711.

Savidge, N. (2016, December 21). Legislators criticize UW-Madison professor's course on race, tweets about shooting of officers. *Wisconsin State Journal*. Retrieved from http://host.madison.com/wsj/news/local/education/university/legislators-criticize-uw-madison-professor-s-course-on-race-tweets/article_b09c432a-6e83-5c96-8cbf-3599503f093c.html.

Sawchuk, S. (2010). States strive to overhaul teacher tenure. *Education Week*, *29*(28), 1–18.

Schein, E. H. (2010). *Organizational culture and leadership* (4th ed.). San Franciso, CA: Jossey-Bass.

Schuster, J. H., & Finkelstein, M. (2006). *The American faculty: The restructuring of academic work and careers*. Baltimore, MD: Johns Hopkins University Press.

Slaughter, S., & Rhoades, G. (2004). *Academic capitalism and the new economy: Markets, state, and higher education*. Baltimore, MD: Johns Hopkins University Press.

Strauss, V. (2015, June 5). Is Gov. Scott Walker putting the University of Wisconsin system in jeopardy? *The Washington Post*. Retrieved from www.washingtonpost.com/news/answer-sheet/wp/2015/06/05/is-gov-scott-walker-putting-the-university-of-wisconsin-system-in-jeopardy/?utm_term=.f712188f5a22

Thornton, S. (2005). Implementing flexible tenure clock policies. *New Directions for Higher Education*, (130), 67–80.

Tierney, W. G., & Bensimon, E. M. (1996). *Promotion and tenure: Community and socialization in academe*. Albany, NY: State University of New York Press.

Tierney, W. G., & Rhoads, R. A. (1994). *Faculty socialization as cultural process: A mirror of institutional commitment*. Washington, DC: The George Washington University, School of Education and Human Development.

Trower, C. A. (2012, November/December). The tenure test. *Trusteeship*. Retrieved from www.agb.org/trusteeship/2012/11/tenure-test

Van Maanen, J., & Schein, E. H. (1979). Toward a theory of organizational socialization. In B. M. Staw & L. L. Cummings (Eds.), *Research in Organizational Behavior* (Vol. 1, pp. 209–264). Greenwich, CT: JAI Press.

Ward, K., & Wolf-Wendel, L. (2004). Fear factor: How safe is it to make time for faculty? *Academe*, *90*(6), 38–31.

Whicker, M. L., Kronenfeld, J. J., & Strickland, R. A. (1993). *Getting tenure*. Thousand Oaks, CA: Sage Publications.

Chapter 2

The Basics of Productivity

168 is a magic number. Whether we're Nobel Prize winning scientists, university presidents, or newly named assistant professors, we all have 168 hours in a week. Peter Higgs won the Nobel Prize in Physics in 2013 for his role in discovering a mechanism that contributes to our understanding of the origin of mass of subatomic particles. After winning his award, he told *The Guardian*, "It's difficult to imagine how I would ever have enough peace and quiet in the present sort of climate to do what I did in 1964" (Aitkenhead, 2013). The challenges facing faculty today result in time pressures dramatically greater than those a generation or two ago (Berg & Seeber, 2016; Finkelstein, Conley, & Schuster, 2016; Gardner & Veliz, 2014; Plater, 1995; Toutkoushian & Bellas, 1999; Zemsky, Wegner, & Massy, 2005). In order to meet the demands of tenure, assistant professors must figure out how to manage daily activities to make progress toward tenure. Often, when advising assistant professors, mentors and experienced faculty encourage pre-tenure faculty to come up with a system for time management. As the advice goes, you need a system of tracking all your to-do list items and balancing all your competing deadlines. Unfortunately, this is horrible advice. Pre-tenure faculty can be excellent at managing time and yet still fall woefully short of meeting the institution's expectations for tenure. It is possible for you to be efficient and complete all tasks on a daily basis. However, if your tasks are largely insignificant to the university and your tenure review committees, then efficiency will provide you little comfort following a negative tenure vote.

Instead of advising efficiency, then, I strongly encourage all faculty, particularly pre-tenure faculty, to become experts in task management, that is managing what you do more than your time or calendar. Focusing on task management offers concrete advantages over traditional time management strategies. First, the likelihood of success when focusing on a task is much greater; you can tackle a task over and over again until you complete it successfully. While you cannot get back an hour of lost time, focusing on tasks helps identify the high priority items needed to gain tenure and provides a means to align daily and weekly activities

27

to strengthen your tenure case. Of course, time is related to task management, and you must allocate time in your schedule for completing tasks. But by orienting yourself around tasks, you can focus on *what* you are doing with your time rather than on time itself. In the end, everyone has the same time resources. You may be at a top research university with nearly bottomless financial resources and stellar graduate research assistants or you may be at a smaller institution with high teaching loads, limited resources, and no graduate students. Regardless of your situation, everyone on the tenure clock has the same 168 hours in any week to complete the necessary tasks.

In order to conceptualize the discussion of productivity in this chapter, it is necessary to think, at least to some degree, about time and faculty work as a zero-sum game (Massy & Zemsky, 1994). Having a fixed amount of time means saying yes to one thing and, by default, saying no to something else. Spending an hour revising your lecture notes means losing an hour to analyze your research data. Staying late in the lab means saying no to your daughter's soccer practice. In many cases, the choice is not between good and bad options, but rather good and better ways to spend your time. When thinking about this issue, consider how the decisions you make on a daily, weekly, or semester basis become a series of trade-offs. One of the best ways to think about our work as faculty is to consider the large and small trade-offs that we make every day, often without thinking about it. Trade-offs exist between the demands of both our professional lives and personal lives.

Trade-offs also play a part in how you consider your role as a professor, balancing teaching, research, service, and administrative tasks. To be clear, there needs to be balance across tasks because faculty have competing roles, but tasks can merge together at least somewhat cohesively (Clark, 1987). The various faculty roles can be integrated and have some overlap (Colbeck, 1998), such as service and teaching or research and teaching, allowing faculty to simultaneously engage across multiple roles (Layzell, 1996). Ultimately, faculty have the agency (Bandura, 1989a) to determine how to allocate priorities, tasks, and time. Unlike many of our staff colleagues on campus, faculty are largely able to decide what work we choose to pursue, how to pursue it, and when we plan to do so. The ability to determine our own priorities, routines, and daily activities represents one of the greatest freedoms of faculty work.

For many faculty, especially assistant professors, time, tasks, and productivity are viewed negatively. Frequently, the only consideration becomes how to squeeze more things into a day. As Gappa, Austin, and Trice (2007) described, "External calls for greater accountability and demonstrable outcomes, institutional pressure for faculty to generate revenue, and the necessity of keeping up with the never-ending expansion of new knowledge all conspire to create seemingly endless demands and expectations on faculty members" (p. 17). There is always another research article to publish or a class lecture to improve. Faculty engage in mental gymnastics to develop justifications to feel better about their time-related decisions. "I have to work late in the office every night—but only while I pursue tenure." "My professional life needs to take priority right now, but it is only temporary." Unfortunately, temporary has a sneaky way of becoming permanent! Truly ask yourself, when was the last time you were not busy? The challenge of busyness rests in feeling like you do not have time to get everything finished and feeling habitually behind. The research literature refers to this feeling as "time famine," and it leads to stress and lower job and life satisfaction (Perlow, 1999).

Paradoxically, the goal of productivity is not about helping you *do more*, in fact, but really about helping you *do less* (McKeown, 2014). Busyness may feel productive, but ultimately it will not help in accomplishing the goal of tenure. Instead, true productivity frees up the resources of time and mental energy to pursue your most important work. Pre-tenure faculty can struggle to understand what matters for tenure and how to balance competing tasks. For scholars of color who often face additional service and mentorship demands, the struggle only increases (Rice, Sorcinelli, & Austin, 2000). My goal is to help think through the ways pre-tenure faculty can filter and schedule commitments based on a priority system that will ultimately help create happy and healthy lives, personally and professionally, while also clearing the bar for tenure. Eliminating everything that stands in the way remains one of the simplest yet most challenging ways to achieve your highest goals.

When Steve Jobs returned to Apple as CEO, the company had lost its way. Jobs turned his notoriously exacting personality to cutting the number of products that Apple created. Discussing his philosophy on focus at the Worldwide Developers Conference in May 1997, Jobs said,

> People think focus is just saying yes to the thing you got to focus on. But that's not what it means at all. It means saying no to the hundred other good ideas that there are. You have to pick carefully. I'm actually as proud of the things we haven't done as the things I have done. Innovation is saying no to 1000 things.
>
> (Gallo, 2016)

I believe this notion can profoundly change the direction of tenure cases and careers. There are little tips and tricks that can be used to enhance efficiency and improve effectiveness. I have included many of these in this chapter. However, these tactical approaches are not real game changers. The real game changer is a shift in approach and attitude toward faculty work. It means considering the trade-offs of a decision before making a commitment, thinking about whether a *good* idea is the *best* idea, and having daily work driven by your highest priorities. No one can create more time on the tenure clock (or in the week), but it is possible to focus on getting the most out of the time available, reducing the stress of the tenure process and, in the end, achieving the goal of tenure.

PAUSE AND REFLECT

What should you say no to in order to focus on your most important priorities? If you were to create a "*Not* To Do" List, what should be on it?

_____

_____

_____

_____

POWER OF FOCUS

Of all the challenges facing pre-tenure faculty, focus may be the most difficult. Most of us intuitively understand that faculty work today, as noted by Professor Higgs at the beginning of this chapter, is different than in the past (Schuster & Finkelstein, 2008). In a knowledge economy, our value and contribution— whether as individual faculty or as institutions—comes from ideas and creativity instead of from producing a widget (Harris & Holley, 2016). The frustration for faculty is, while everyone agrees that ideas, innovation, and creativity are immensely valuable, email, paperwork, and meetings drain our time and fail to add value to daily work. Moreover, research has found that these activities drain a significant amount of time both during and between semesters (Bentley & Kyvik, 2013). To push against this trend, Georgetown computer science professor Cal Newport has suggested that the goal of faculty and other knowledge workers should be *deep work*. In his book (Newport, 2016), he advances this notion of deep work: focused work that occurs in a distraction-free environment and brings value. The central premise of his book is that too often we focus on shallow work, which creates a false sense of productivity.

Deep professional work activities performed in a state of distraction-free concentration can push the limits of your cognitive capabilities. In contrast, shallow work is not cognitively demanding and is often performed while distracted. Furthermore, shallow work, while relatively easy to complete, holds very little value to your career or to society more broadly. For faculty, deep work might include research discoveries, data analysis, or writing—all activities that directly lead to tenure, professional recognition, and advancing the discipline.

It is human nature to follow what Newport calls the principle of least resistance. Simply put, without clear and immediate feedback on the impact of their behaviors, people will tend toward those that are easiest in the moment. For instance, responding to an email requires less cognitive effort than advancing your conceptual understanding of a new methodological technique in your discipline.

TABLE 2.1 Deep and Shallow Faculty Work

Deep Work	Shallow Work
Designing research studies	Checking email
Learning new research method	Filling out annual review paperwork
Analyzing data	Working on references for an article
Writing books and journal articles	Creating PowerPoint slides for class
Developing lectures and class activities	Updating your CV
Grading research papers	Completing IRB application
Reviewing manuscripts	Attending committee meetings

You will naturally be drawn to responding to the email because it is less demanding and has the immediate feedback of deleting the email from your inbox. Understanding this concept is critically important for pre-tenure faculty and directly relates to the priorities and task management approaches mentioned earlier in this chapter.

The activities and work necessary for achievements in tenure generally, and research specifically, often come without immediate feedback. Faculty constantly have to focus on activities with long-term rewards but which lack immediate feedback. Unfortunately, because of this principle, pre-tenure faculty tend to focus on areas where they are likely to get immediate feedback rather than on those most significant to tenure and future career aspirations. For example, your department chair may immediately acknowledge your work on a department committee; the feedback provides you a sense of satisfaction, reward, and positive reinforcement. Sadly, there is no one sitting around waiting to praise the important edits just completed on a manuscript. One of your biggest challenges

---

PAUSE AND REFLECT

What type of shallow work do you tend to do most? When you need to focus on a difficult task, what are you most likely to do instead to give the appearance of productivity?

_____

_____

_____

_____

as an assistant professor is to avoid the temptation of doing what comes easiest. Instead, you have to persevere and focus on the difficult work that is ultimately rewarded in the tenure and promotion process (Hart & Cress, 2008).

Similarly, the lack of a clear and agreed upon definition of productivity often leads to busyness as a proxy for productivity. Those who are quick to respond to emails, always volunteer to help out on committees, and spend time bouncing new research ideas off colleagues are seen as busy and productive, right? The truth can be exactly the opposite. Much of the emphasis on time management for assistant professors is about how we can complete shallow work more quickly and efficiently. To be sure, there is no way to eliminate shallow work entirely from our professional lives (trust me, I have tried). When you have to spend some time on the administrative minutiae of faculty work, you need to be efficient in getting these items off of your to-do list. Nevertheless, a successful tenure case and a fulfilling academic career rests on a dedication to deep work.

IMPORTANCE OF ROUTINES AND RITUALS

One of the best ways to incorporate deep work into daily activities is through routines and rituals, which make the daily grind much smoother (Graybiel, 2008). We often think about this in the context of writing. You may have your favorite table at the coffee shop or particular music to help get you into the mood to write. This same notion holds for deep work. In his seminal work on faculty productivity and writing, Robert Boice (1990) described detailed procedures for ensuring productive writing. He found that faculty could support regular writing through rituals such as arranging a regular writing place, charting progress, and scheduling writing during alert parts of the day, rather than in the late evening. At the core of his advice and supported by the psychology literature (Heath & Heath, 2010) is the notion of utilizing rituals to guide daily practice rather than relying on willpower each time productivity is needed.

Rituals and routines provide an order and predictability to life; indeed, it is difficult to imagine a world completely devoid of them. Routines organize time and activities by providing a sequence to follow or a manual (Ehn & Lofgren, 2009) of how you can engage in your faculty work. Rituals move beyond routines by ascribing a meaning or significance to an action (Graybiel, 2008). One example of the power of rituals is how they bring comfort and the hope of a desired outcome to work (Deal & Kennedy, 2000; Dunn, 2000). For instance, rituals in faculty work can set expectations for behavior. Before teaching class, for example, you may have a ritual of getting a cup of coffee and walking around the quad, which helps you mentally prepare and gets you into the proper mindset for teaching. In the context of productivity, rituals can be useful in establishing what you will do and how you will do it.

32

PAUSE AND REFLECT

What routines and rituals do you currently use and how do these help set you up for success?

_____

_____

_____

What aspects of your faculty work might need some new routines or rituals?

_____

_____

_____

Are there routines or rituals that are not helping and should be replaced with better ones?

_____

_____

_____

Increasing the amount of time spent on deep work requires embracing boredom in order to avoid distraction. Like most people, I hate to be bored. Technology today makes avoiding boredom quite easy. Waiting in line at the grocery store quickly becomes interesting with a quick glance at Facebook. Podcasts, an audiobook, or NPR are at the click of a button during my commute. I can always be doing something and technology helps me stay busy. Sadly, busyness is the enemy of deep work. Newport convincingly argues the need to embrace boredom. During states of boredom, our minds are able to wander and contemplate big ideas that may be difficult to conceptualize during deep work sessions. In ways we are just beginning to understand, new advances in neuroscience and cognitive psychology suggest that the brain processes information outside of focused work sessions (Goleman, 2013; Kahneman, 2013; Pink, 2005). For example, we often get great ideas in the shower because it is one of the few times our minds are not occupied by social media, the news, or some other distraction.

The technology constantly surrounding us presents wonderful opportunities for achieving academic work. Yet, we must also understand the ways in which technology trains our minds to avoid cognitively demanding tasks. Case in point: Research into heavy media multitaskers—people who consume more than one stream of media at the same time—found these individuals were more susceptible

33

to distraction and had worse working memory (Ophir, Nass, & Wagner, 2009). While watching a sporting event, it is possible to have my phone out checking stats online and seeing what fans are saying on Twitter. Television shows do not demand much attention, so why not pay bills while watching? We are fooled into thinking we are great at multitasking. We think we can watch a ballgame, check stats online, follow Twitter, check Facebook, and pay bills all at the same time. What's the big deal? The problem is that these kinds of activities train our brains to crave distraction. How do I expect to focus for two or three hours on analyzing my data when I have trained my brain every night at home to expect a new stimulus every five seconds? Fighting against these distractions is a constant battle for me. What distractions do you struggle with right now? Are you on Facebook, Twitter, or Instagram too frequently? Do you waste time searching for things on Amazon? What are the sources of distraction that you need to work on limiting?

Our goal for productivity should be learning tactics and strategies to help focus on high priorities and deep work activities. After all, achievements in these areas present the most important work of a faculty career and a tenure bid. No one will be perfect in maximizing deep work time, minimizing shallow work, and allocating time and effort towards the most important priorities. But successfully navigating the road to tenure and productivity is a continual process that anyone can work at improving, just as you work at getting better at teaching or using a research method. I strongly encourage pre-tenure faculty to spend time, effort, and energy thinking about the processes underlying faculty work. Whether you follow the advice offered here or utilize other helpful sources and systems of productivity out there, one of the best ways to promote a successful tenure case is to improve your process of faculty work. It may seem counterintuitive to spend precious pre-tenure time on philosophical ideas such as goal setting and contemplating how to improve productivity. In reality, however, this effort could move the needle in a positive direction for a tenure case more than any other. Establishing what to work on, how to work on it, and how to let priorities drive daily work will provide the necessary and essential foundation for a successful tenure case.

EFFECTIVE GOAL SETTING

Every January gyms, weight-loss programs, and sellers of exercise equipment have an explosion of interest as people set their New Year's resolutions. By the end of January, the gym empties and the treadmill collects laundry. Resolutions, sadly, tend to be unsuccessful. Only 46 percent of people making New Year's resolutions successfully maintain their goals by July 1 (Norcross, Mrykalo, & Blagys, 2002). Unfortunately, the same thing occurs every August as academics set their academic New Year's resolutions upon returning to campus. More sobering, a desire to change even professionally does not lead to success in keeping resolutions. Instead, Norcross and colleagues (2002) found that positive strategies, such as stimulus control (differences in behaviors from various inputs and environments), positive thinking, and reinforcement management (the process of increasing a desirable behavior), propelled deep work forward.

Many faculty believe goal setting to be either a waste of time or another administrative burden, but research consistently demonstrates the power of goals to improve performance. Research on goal setting for students, for example, has yielded positive results. Multiple extensive studies have shown that, for students, goals increase achievement, with correlational and experimental results revealing that goals increase success rates in education (Harackiewicz, Barron, Tauer, & Elliot, 2002; Latham & Locke, 2007; Locke & Latham, 1990). When considering the influence of the tenure process on goal setting, the literature raises questions of how pre-tenure faculty members frame goals. Drach-Zahavy and Erez (2002) found lower performance in faculty who viewed difficult goals as threats versus new challenges. Setting goals has also been shown to increase motivation. For example, the literature from industrial/organizational psychology consistently finds that giving someone a specific goal versus telling them to do their best increases motivation (Latham & Locke, 2007). Along with self-efficacy, task specific confidence (Bandura, 1989b) and goals often influence other important variables such as personality or monetary incentives.

Given this finding, utilizing the SMART goal setting method for both tenure and life more generally can improve your preparation for tenure. The SMART goal method establishes a clear approach to the goal, identifies action items, and measures progress toward achievement (Conzemius & O'Neill, 2005; Doran, 1981; Shahin & Mahbod, 2007). The method incorporates a series of examples reflecting the effective articulation of SMART goals. You must be able to specifically identify an action in order to fully reap the benefits of the method.

BIG HAIRY AUDACIOUS GOAL

Before moving on to operationalizing goals, I want to give a word of note about stretch goals—goals that push the limits of one's ability (Kerr & Landauer, 2004; Kerr & LePelley, 2013). Safe and attainable goals, such as SMART goals, are doable with your existing capability. You need safe goals that move you closer to successfully receiving tenure. However, you also need to set Big Hairy Audacious Goals, or BHAG. Noted business researcher James C. Collins described a BHAG as an organization-wide goal that helped businesses craft their long-term vision (Collins, 1999, 2001). The best BHAGs help create processes and systems for achievement while stretching the mind to think bigger and reach farther. Collins suggested that BHAGs have about a 50–70 percent chance of success (Collins, 2001). No one would want all of the goals for tenure to have a 50 percent chance of success, but having one (or possibly two) BHAGs can push you to think outside

S—Specific: Goal needs to be specific.

Weak: Write an article.
Better: Write an article on investing in emerging markets for the Journal of Finance.

M—Measurable: Goal needs to be measurable. Without a measurable goal, you will not know when you have achieved your goal or how to evaluate your progress.

Weak: I want to focus on writing this year.
Better: I want to write for at least one hour per day, five days per week.

A—Attainable: Goal needs to be attainable. It is okay to create some reach goals and there is no need to complete every goal on the list. But, as an example, I should not make a goal of playing Major League Baseball. I am slow, do not hit the ball very far, and am generally uncoordinated. I have zero chance of achieving the goal of becoming a major leaguer.

Weak: Win the Nobel Prize.
Better: Publish an article in the top journal in my field.

R—Relevant: Goal should be based on key areas of life. For professional goals, consider the expectations for tenure both in your discipline generally and your institution specifically.

Weak: I want to serve on a time-intensive committee even though service won't be a factor in my tenure.
Better: I want to publish in my field's top journal, which will strengthen my tenure case.

T—Time limited: Goal should be time bound. An open-ended goal is much more difficult to accomplish than one with a clear deadline.

Weak: I want to publish a book.
Better: I want to submit a book proposal by July 1.

WORKSHEET 2.1 CREATE A SMART GOAL

Now give it a try using the following template. *S—Specific, M—Measureable, A—Attainable, R—Relevant, T—Time limited.*

S—Specific. Goal needs to be specific. What do you want to achieve? (Hint: Focus on a detailed outcome.)

_____

_____

M—Measurable. Goal needs to be measurable. How do you plan to measure your goal? (Hint: Think numbers. Example: 3 papers written or 40 hours of writing a month, etc.)

_____

_____

How will you know you have completed your goal? (Hint: Describe what success looks like.)

_____

_____

A—Attainable. Goal needs to be attainable. Brainstorm what challenges might prevent you from completing your goal.

_____

_____

Considering what you listed above, is your goal still attainable? If yes, describe how you will overcome these challenges. If not, revisit your goal and start with S.

_____

_____

R—Relevant. Goal should be based on key area of your life. For professional goals, how does the goal help you get tenure?

_____

_____

T—Time. Goal should be time bound.
When will you start working on your goal?
_____(Date)

When will you complete your goal?
_____(Date)

the box in ways that develop your work into the national standard many institutions want to see in tenure candidates. A BHAG is perfect to challenge one's thinking and consider different approaches to academic work. Depending on the situation, the particulars of the BHAG will vary, but could include things like a large federal research grant, writing an op-ed in *The New York Times*, or being named as the outstanding early career scholar award for a professional association. The power of this type of goal is that it provides the motivation of an achievable goal, yet it forces you to develop different systems of working. Just the process of pursuing a BHAG can lead you to breakthroughs that may not have occurred—even if you never actually reach the Big Hairy Audacious Goal.

MAKE A PLAN

Goals can be helpful in planning, but a single goal alone does not constitute a plan. For both the academic year and for the tenure probationary period, pre-tenure faculty should come up with a set of SMART goals. Since these goals are time sensitive, you should be able to work backwards to determine plans for each month, week, and day to make sure you complete them. Breaking a goal down into manageable sections allows for a less intimidating workload. At the beginning of each month, take an hour to think through professional goals that will require your attention during the next thirty days. Then, at the beginning of each week, consider what needs to be accomplished in that time frame. By taking the time to plan each month and week, you will be in a much better position to make progress on each of the key goals for tenure.

TOO BUSY AND TOO STRESSED

I bet every time you walk across campus and run into a colleague, the conversation goes something like this: "Hi, how's it going?" "Good, I'm just so busy." "Yep, me too! It must be that time of the semester." It does not matter when this conversation occurs. It is *always* "that time" of the semester. The curse of knowledge work is that it can be done at anytime and pretty much anywhere. Too often, this turns into all the time and everywhere. While it may be impossible to compare the stress of faculty today with that of previous generations, research on stress in academia suggests that busyness and work stress are almost a "necessary kind of comfort discourse, a tranquilizer to cope with the diversity of competing messages about truth in this world, and the dreadful uncertainty of our times" (Newton, 1999, p. 249). The stress of faculty life in general, and pursuing tenure specifically, can be difficult to manage. As noted in Chapter 1, the tenure process presents challenges for faculty in navigating issues of climate and culture along with the other pressures inherent in the process (Trower, 2012). In the end, the stress and busyness discourse reassures us by normalizing stress and providing solidarity with others facing stress and pressure. If everyone feels this way, it can be oddly reassuring.

In a study that garnered attention from faculty by validating longstanding concerns and quantifying the "reality" of the stress discourse, John Ziker (2014) of Boise State University found that faculty at Boise dedicated 61 work hours per week to faculty work, with nearly 30 percent of their time occupied by administrative tasks. Other studies (Bentley & Kyvik, 2013; Kyvik, 2013a, 2013b) have found that faculty work far more than the standard 40-hour work-week. In an examination of faculty life across 13 countries, Bentley and Kyvik (2013) found that faculty at U.S. colleges and universities worked 51.4 hours per week during the semester (20.7 hours for teaching, 14.6 hours for research, 8 hours for administration, and 8.1 hours for service and other academic work). During non-teaching periods, faculty still spent time on teaching (8.3 hours), research (24.1 hours), administration (9.6 hours), and service and other academic work (5.7 hours), for a total of 47.7 hours per week. The reality is that faculty today work a tremendous number of hours across all areas of responsibility.

In light of the pressures for increased accountability at colleges and universities (Burke, 2005), faculty work faces fundamental challenges that simply did not exist for past generations. Teaching, research, and service have all become increasingly complex and specialized. At the same time, higher education faces substantial budget cuts, meaning that resources to support faculty work have declined—particularly since the Great Recession in 2008 (Finkelstein et al., 2016). Regardless of the type of institution you work at today, faculty responsibilities have become blurred (Schuster & Finkelstein, 2008). Faculty at research universities spend more time on teaching than they used to, while faculty at teaching institutions spend more time on research and scholarly activities than they did historically. It is important to note, however, that workload, compensation, and reward policies are hardly uniform across institutions (Fairweather, 2002). In some cases, faculty receive additional compensation for teaching higher course loads, while in other situations, faculty get an increased salary for producing scholarly work even if the institution primarily focuses on teaching (Fairweather, 2000). Ultimately, the research clearly demonstrates that pressures for increased faculty productivity have increased in recent years as faculty feel pressure and the need to perform (Berg & Seeber, 2016). The challenge for faculty becomes balancing competing demands in an environment of constrained resources.

The literature clearly documents the pressures facing faculty, as well as the increased complexity of academic work (Colbeck, 1998; Gappa et al., 2007; Rice et al., 2000). As Rhoades (2009) described, pre-tenure faculty today are "expected to publish more, generate more grants, teach more students in more contexts, and be responsive 24/7" (p. 56). I do not think this is quite right. At the individual level, faculty do not have *too much* work to do. Rather, I think the issue is that faculty fail to follow a carefully crafted and organized schedule. Calendars, to-do lists, and email are tools that assist in professional work: They serve us; we do not serve them. Yet, too often, the urgent and insignificant tasks that confront us on a daily basis can crowd out the important and significant work that should be our primary focus. As Parkinson's Law states, "work expands so as to fill the time available for its completion." Simply put, you will be busy, but not necessarily productive. Unfortunately, the culture of higher education has come to glorify the concept of *busy*. Many faculty members blame themselves for not managing their work better, but are not able to change their approach (Jacobs, 2004). This is not healthy. Not only will your mental and physical health suffer, but no one can successfully engage in their best work 60+ hours per week. Too many pre-tenure faculty struggle with heavy workloads that are time consuming and draining (Menges, 1999). This concern is particularly acute for pre-tenure faculty with families, aging parents, health challenges, and additional responsibilities at home (Wolf-Wendel & Ward, 2006).

POWER AND POTENTIAL OF A WEEKLY TEMPLATE

As faculty members, we have tremendous flexibility in how we schedule our time. Each week there are only a few appointments that we absolutely must attend, including class and office hours. Having this opportunity to arrange daily activities represents one of the great freedoms of faculty life. The ability to determine how to spend time can be powerful yet debilitating. No matter how much work we do, there is always more to be done. There is always another article to write, another email to send, or more tweaking needed for next week's class. We work in dynamic and active disciplines where there is always more to discover.

Even simple questions—What time does the workday start? What time does it end? What days *are* workdays?—often have unclear answers. Time and attention must be distributed in a way that boosts productivity yet maintains sanity. Indeed, overwhelmed and anxious feelings pervade among assistant professors and stem from a failure to make decisions about scheduling and committing to those decisions. Let's be honest: Most deans, department chairs, and students will not tell faculty to work less. We must advocate for ourselves.

How can you avoid falling into the trap of working constantly? My biggest asset has been a weekly schedule template. A template can help you stay focused on your most important work and reset your schedule each week. No week will ever go exactly according to the template, but a schedule can keep you pointed in the right direction. In particular, a weekly template monitors commitment levels when scheduling meetings weeks ahead of time. If you already have several advising appointments filling up your calendar in a given week, you will know you need to push another meeting to the following week. This helps balance all your priorities.

STEPS FOR CREATING A WEEKLY TEMPLATE

Step 1. Determine your start and end time each day.

As you can see from my template below, I generally begin my workday at 8:30 am and end at 5 pm. I have young kids to drop off at school, and I want to be home in time for dinner each evening. Conversely, I have a colleague who is a night owl; her workday starts at noon and ends around 9 pm. It does not really matter what hours you choose, but I encourage you to set a start and stop time to balance your work and personal life.

Step 2. Add up how many hours you will work each week.

From Monday to Friday, I have 40 hours of work scheduled with 30 minutes for lunch every day. I spend about two hours on the weekend catching up on email and planning my upcoming week for a total of 42 hours per week. I rarely work outside of these hours. When I first started on the tenure track, I fell into the trap of working all the time. However, over time, I began to realize that I did not need to do this to be successful and began structuring my work weeks better. To be sure, then and now, there are weeks when I have a major deadline and I put in more time, but generally I stick to my 42 hours. If you prioritize your work as I have advised in this chapter (i.e., prioritizing tasks, balancing demands, etc.) and stay focused on the things that will help you get tenure, you can largely avoid the trap of working 60+ hours. It is simply not true, as Tierney and Bensimon (1996) heard from a pre-tenure faculty member, that "the more overworked you were, the better faculty person you were" (p. 60). While this sentiment prevails across higher education, you can fight against this trend and still have a successful case for tenure and promotion.

Step 3. Determine your major work areas and the percentage of time to be allocated to each area.

Assistant professors must balance competing demands, often failing to identify their major areas of responsibility. To guard against this, David Allen's (2015) Getting Things Done (GTD) method can be useful. GTD treats your major areas of responsibility as contexts; for example, most faculty have teaching, research, and service as major areas. Others may have additional major areas such as a grant project or an administrative role. I also suggest adding an area for administrative work. Even if you do not have a formal administrative role, administrative items— from annual faculty reports to email correspondence—will require completion. Most assistant professors have between 4–6 major areas of responsibility.

Now that you've identified your areas, determine the percentage of time you should allocate to each area. On research, will you spend 25 percent of your time or 50 percent? Will teaching be 30 percent or 20 percent? Obviously, this will vary based on your teaching load as discussed in Chapter 1. Generally, you can start by allocating percentages based on your teaching load and then adjust based on your particular situation. For example, if you are teaching a class for the first time, you may allocate more time for planning and preparation. If you have taught a class multiple times, you can probably afford to allocate some of your teaching percentage to other areas. Moreover, if you know that your institution's tenure process does not place much weight on teaching, research can be your primary focus. Of course, in this case you will not put teaching at zero or five percent, but it would be a mistake if your percentages do not align generally with the institution's tenure expectations. Everyone's percentage will be slightly different. Setting this percentage before the semester begins gives you the opportunity to adjust your time appropriately before being confronted with the daily pressures of work that will come up in the middle of the semester.

Step 4. Calculate the number of hours to be spent on each major work area.

Now that you have the number of hours to work each week and the percentages to allocate to each major work area, simply multiply the hours by each percentage. You may have to finesse it a little to get round numbers, but refrain from substantially changing the hours for each area. Remember, the reason you set those work hours and percentages independently from seeing how many hours you are going to assign to each major area is to keep your working hours under control. For first timers, you may find yourself shocked at how much or how little you should spend on each of the areas of responsibility. If you spent your time differently in the past, reflect on why this was the case. I have a hunch it is because you spent too much time on less significant areas while at the same time neglecting areas that are most important for getting tenure. I know that was certainly true for me early in my career.

Step 5. Schedule the hours for each area within the start and stop times you determined in Step 1.

I know what you are thinking: I can add a few more hours here and there and get even more done. Resist this temptation! You do not need to work more. Trust your system and schedule the hours you determined you *needed* in the prior steps. As you follow each step, consider your variance in energy level during the course of the day. Consider standing meetings and other obligations that require your time. After teaching class, I know that I am not going to have the mental energy to write a new manuscript, so that is a perfect time for responding to email or to schedule an advising meeting that I can undertake with less mental energy. I also build in time for lunch every day to give myself a break. It may seem counterproductive to take time out of the middle of the day, but I promise that taking a break will help you return refreshed for the afternoon. By taking the break, you may work less time overall, but you will be even more productive than if you tried to slog through the day without a pause.

	Sunday	Monday	Tuesday	Wednesday	Thursday	Friday	Saturday
8:30		8:30 AM Class Prep	8:30 AM Research	8:30 AM Class Prep	8:30 AM Research	8:30 AM Class Prep	
9:00							
9:30							
10:00		10 AM Class 1		10 AM Class 1		10 AM Class 1	
10:30							
11:00		Email		Email		Email	
11:30		11:30 AM Service/Meetings	Email	11:30 AM Research		11:30 AM Research	
12:00					Email		
12:30		Lunch	Lunch	Lunch	Lunch	Lunch	
1:00		1 PM Research	1 PM Class Prep	1 PM Office Hours/ Teaching	1 PM Class Prep	1 PM Research	
1:30							
2:00			2 PM Class 2		2 PM Class 2		
2:30							
3:00	3 PM Weekly Planning/ Email					3 PM Weekly review	
3:30			3:30 PM Service/Meetings		3:30 PM Service/Meeting		
4:00						4 PM Email	
4:30	Email	Email	Email	Email	Email		

FIGURE 2.1 Weekly Schedule Template

WORKSHEET 2.2 CREATE YOUR OWN WEEKLY TEMPLATE

The following steps will help you develop your own weekly template.

Step 1. Determine your work day start and end time:

Start Time: _____

End Time: _____

Step 2. Calculate how many hours to work each week.

Number of work hours per day:

A

Number of work days each week:

B

A	×	B	=	C

Total Number of Work Hours

Step 3. List your major areas of work and the percentage of time allocated to each.

Major Work Area	Percentage of Your Time
	%
	%
	%
	%
	%
TOTAL	100%

WORKSHEET 2.2 Continued

Step 4. Calculate the number of hours to be spent on each major work area

Major Work Area	Percentage of Your Time		Number of Work Hours (C from Step 1)	Hours for Work Area
	%	x		
	%	x		
	%	x		
	%	x		
	%	x		
TOTAL	100%	x		

Step 5. Schedule the hours for each area with the start and end times from Step 1 in the Sample Weekly Calendar Template.

Sample Weekly Calendar Template

Time	Sun.	Mon.	Tue.	Wed.	Thurs.	Fri.	Sat.
5:00AM							
6:00							
7:00							
8:00							
9:00							
10:00							
11:00							
12:00PM							
1:00							
2:00							
3:00							
4:00							
5:00							
6:00							
7:00							
8:00							
9:00							
10:00							
11:00							
12:00AM							

Total Hours Planned to Work

Invest Time to Improve How You Spend Your Time

In order to create my own weekly schedule template, I spend about two hours at the start of each semester working through the process. Taking two hours at this time may seem like a lot, but you will spend more time trying to reinvent the wheel each week during the semester. Without a clear template, human nature tends to direct plans; this makes it much more likely that each week will be based on what seems most urgent in the moment rather than on the items that lead to tenure.

MONSTER IN THE EMAIL INBOX

Email serves as a powerful communications tool. Yet I suspect that, for faculty, few things prove a greater source of frustration. From student messages to administrative requests, it can seem that very little good news comes in the form of email. Messages can easily derail your day. Even the best laid plans for grading papers or making progress on your latest manuscript can be undone by an email emergency. And even non-emergency email can prove dangerous. A better way to think about email is death by 1,000 cuts. Email can slice up your day and serve as a constant distraction, leaving you few precious minutes to focus on the things that will get you tenure.

For many people, the email inbox serves as their to-do list, filing cabinet, and junk drawer all in one. Too often, we forget the true purpose of an email inbox, which is simply a place for messages to initially land and be processed. Do you have more than 50 messages in your inbox right now? 100? 500? More? I don't even want to know! For your own sanity, I suggest you gain control of your inbox. Truthfully, no one gets tenure because they are quick to respond to messages. Nevertheless, failing to get an inbox under control can severely hamper your tenure case. With the time pressures of tenure and of faculty life in general, you do not need the hassle of a chaotic email inbox. Fortunately, there are a few simple steps you can enact to help manage your email and even reduce the number of messages you receive on a daily basis.

1. Check Your Email Less

I have a phone in my office. I do not know its number, and I rarely get calls on it. Yet, if there is an emergency, I almost always receive a phone call. Even more likely, my department administrative assistant will probably send a quick text letting me know that something needs my attention. Even in today's digital age, few truly urgent emergencies come via email. Even so, when email notifications constantly pop-up, email exerts control over you, and over tenure. Just because someone wants to get in touch with you does not mean they get to interrupt your carefully planned schedule. Think about it: If you stop your work to answer an email as soon as it arrives, you are implying that your work is not important. While I would not suggest anyone develop a reputation as someone who never responds to emails from students, administrators, or colleagues, I instead advocate a compromise between never responding to email and checking email constantly. Check your email three or four times per day—personally, I try to check mine morning, midday, and in the late afternoon. This allows me to stay on top of my email, respond to any immediate needs, and yet keep email from dominating my entire day. More often than not, I can knock out my messages in about 15 minutes by checking three times a day. While there are days I am in my email much more, generally limiting my time allows me to be responsive and focus on my top priorities for the day.

2. Delay Sending Emails

Various email programs have different options to achieve this goal, but I rarely send a message as soon as I complete it. Instead, I set the email to send in a few hours or, typically in the case of students, the next day. My goal in this is to train anyone who emails me to expect that they will not get an immediate response. I find this particularly helpful with students because it teaches them not to expect instantaneous responses, which I suspect reduces how many emails they send to me in the first place. Instead of asking me a quick question that is answered on the syllabus because they know they can get in touch with me, my students are forced to seek other sources of information and only contact me when I am the best source for answering their questions.

3. Do Not Use Email as a To-Do List

Whether you prefer to use a paper to-do list or software program, do not use your email for this purpose. Leaving a message in your inbox because the message contains something that needs to be done is not the best approach to manage your to-do list. Not only does it clutter up your inbox, it also increases your stress every time you check your email. Email programs are not designed to help you prioritize your work. Instead, any action items you need to complete from an email should be added to your regular to-do list and prioritized appropriately in the context of other items you need to complete.

Manage Your Email, Do Not Let it Manage You

With email, you can quickly contact co-authors from around the world or answer quick questions from students. However, email also has the potential to keep you from your highest priorities and hurt your pursuit of tenure. When you sit down to prepare your tenure dossier, I promise that you will not wish you had spent more time responding to or sending emails. The tenure process is stressful enough without an overflowing inbox. It may seem like email takes up a fairly small part of the day, but it can quickly grow out of control. I strongly suggest taking steps to reduce the amount of email you send and receive. This is something that most faculty struggle with, and improving your email management can offer a distinct advantage during the tenure process.

ELUSIVE WORK–LIFE BALANCE

As a new faculty member, I dreamed of achieving work–life balance. I would attend conferences, read advice columns in the *Chronicle of Higher Education*, and speak with mentors—all of whom discussed work–life balance. It seemed to be this magical, zen-like situation in which all the pressures, demands, and issues I faced in my daily work suddenly dissolved away. Of course, work–life balance is nothing of the sort. When you are early in your career and trying to make a mark, have a young family, and attempt to have interests outside of academe, balance can seem little more than a mirage always glimmering in the distance.

As I came to understand my role as a faculty member, I began to better comprehend the notion of work–life balance. I started to focus on the word "balance." For years, my friends suggested I try yoga. Having never tried it before, I did not understand how doing a few stretches could be a good workout. However, after trying a few classes, I came to realize the enormous strength, coordination, and even power it took to complete even rudimentary poses. For example, there is the tree pose, where you stand on one leg with the foot of your other leg resting on your inner thigh. The pose is a fairly beginner move, yet just balancing on one leg can be quite the challenge (at least for a novice like me). It would take me a minute, but I could get in the pose without too much trouble. Then, the challenge would start. I would feel stable but, as the seconds ticked by, the real work would begin. My leg would start to wobble and I would have to engage my core just to keep from falling over. I would engage an incredible number of muscles just to maintain a fairly simple pose such as standing on one leg. Work–life balance works the same way. Work–life balance is dynamic, ever-changing, and incredibly complicated. To achieve balance, we all have to make constant corrections to try to stay in line. Moreover, balance is a continual process. When you are in the tree pose, you never complete the pose. You are constantly working to try to hold and maintain the pose for a particular length of time. Not only that, but balance does not happen by accident. It takes intentional effort—both physical and mental—to try to maintain.

Throughout this chapter, I discussed a variety of ways to become more effective and efficient during the pre-tenure years. The goal here is neither effectiveness nor efficiency for its own sake. Rather, the goal is to dedicate time to achieving professional work as well as to your pursuits outside of higher education. One of the keys to achieving this goal is managing expectations—yours, your colleagues', friends', and family's. Setting boundaries and managing expectations are critical to you achieving work–life balance. Establishing priorities, creating a schedule, and utilizing the other strategies in this chapter can help.

If you do not establish your own rules, someone else will establish them for you—or criticize the decisions you make. As Merlin Mann, the productivity guru, once said, "people always despise you if you end up doing less stupid BS than they choose to suffer" (Jones, 2011). Everyone wants to be a good colleague, parent, and spouse but, as an assistant professor, you are the only person most responsible for building a successful tenure case. You need to be honest with yourself and know when you are in a crunch period. Only you are able to determine when you need to spend more time in the office or lab and when you need to get home to see your family or spend time with friends. You are responsible for fulfilling the responsibilities that you have at work and home.

If this is an area in which you struggle, wholesale change will be incredibly difficult. Just as it takes a long time to turn a large ship, it will take a long time to adjust work habits that may have been years in the making. The literature on habits describes a process for changing them (Duhigg, 2012). At the most basic level, a habit is a cue that leads to a routine that leads to a reward. The challenge for changing habits is to keep the same cue and reward but change the routine in the middle. Of course, changing a routine is quite difficult as evidenced, for example, by the number of people who struggle to quit smoking. However, people can change their habits by considering their cues and rewards and finding more healthy and productive routines to replace ineffective ones.

Ultimately, knowing how habits work alone cannot change how you work. You need to believe in your ability to change the ways you work, including how you spend your time and allocate your efforts. For example, if you do not believe you need to find a balance between work and life outside of work, you are obviously not going to find balance. I know what some of you are thinking, because I thought the same thing for many years: The time on the tenure clock flies, and you can just suck it up for a few years—these critical few years. After tenure, there will be time for work–life balance and non-academic pursuits. You need look no further than the number of faculty who have children immediately following tenure to know the pervasiveness of this view. I get it. However, it is critical to understand the toll that this attitude takes. Burnout is defined as "a state of physical, emotional and mental exhaustion caused by long-term involvement in situations that are emotionally demanding" (Harrison, 1999, p. 25). Certainly, assistant professors on the tenure-track are more susceptible to burnout (Lackritz, 2004).

I have always strived to be a professor who is available to my students. One of the reasons I pursued a faculty career is because I enjoy playing a role in my

49

students' intellectual, professional, and personal growth. When I was in my fourth year on the tenure track, a group of students approached me about creating a brown bag lunch series and asked if I would coordinate it. I thought a series of this type would be wonderful for our students and improve the intellectual life of my department. Unfortunately, I had to tell them no. As much as I thought it was a valuable idea and something I hoped they'd be able to accomplish, I knew I would not be able to assist them. I was at a critical point in my tenure process and I needed to dedicate my time professionally to those areas of my work that would be rewarded during my tenure review. At the same time, I had two young children who needed, and deserved, my attention at home.

As I think back to this episode, I do not remember the subject of the brown bag series or if they ended up creating it. Saying no to the group of students was not natural for me. Now, with the benefit of tenure behind me, it is something I would most likely pursue. But in those precious years before tenure, I could not take it on without giving up something else. Since I could not afford to give up my teaching or research time, this service work would have had to come out of somewhere else. I knew it would come out of time that I would spend with friends, time that I would spend exercising, or time that I would sit and roll a ball back and forth with my young children.

I love academic work. I love the intellectual challenge. I love the way I get to answer questions that are interesting to me and work with students who also find them interesting. But at the end of the day, I am no good to anyone—not myself, not my students, not my family—if all I am is a professor. I take pride in my professional work and accomplishments, but they are not all I am. Even years after tenure, this is something I remind myself. If this is an area where you struggle, start small. Try one thing to help achieve a better balance. You do not have to start with the hardest yoga pose, but start with a simple one. The work of improving as an academic is something most of us have been working at our entire lives.

REFERENCES

Aitkenhead, D. (2013, December 6). Peter Higgs: I wouldn't be productive enough for today's academic system. *The Guardian*. Retrieved from www.theguardian.com/science/2013/dec/06/peter-higgs-boson-academic-system

Allen, D. (2015). *Getting things done: The art of stress-free productivity*. New York: Penguin Books.

Bandura, A. (1989a). Human agency in social cognitive theory. *American Psychologist*, *44*(9), 1175–1184.

Bandura, A. (1989b). Self-regulation of motivation and action through internal standards and goal systems. In L. A. Pervin (Ed.), *Goal concepts in personality and social psychology* (pp. 19–85). Hillsdale, NJ: Erlbaum.

Bentley, P. J., & Kyvik, S. (2013). Individual differences in faculty research time allocations across 13 countries. *Research in Higher Education*, *54*(3), 329–348.

Berg, M., & Seeber, B. (2016). *The slow professor: Challenging the culture of speed in the academy*. Toronto: University of Toronto Press.

Boice, R. (1990). *Professors as writers: A self-help guide to productive writing*. Stillwater, OK: New Forums.

Burke, J. C. (2005). *Achieving accountability in higher education: Balancing public, academic, and market demands*. San Francisco, CA: Jossey-Bass.

Clark, B. R. (1987). *The academic life: Small worlds, different worlds*. Princeton, NJ: Carnegie Foundation for the Advancement of Teaching.

Colbeck, C. L. (1998). Merging in a seamless blend: How faculty integrate teaching and research. *Journal of Higher Education*, *69*(6), 647–671.

Collins, J. (1999). Turning goals into results: The power of catalytic mechanisms. *Harvard Business Review*, *77*(4), 70–82.

Collins, J. (2001). *Good to great: Why some companies make the leap and others don't*. New York: HarperCollins Publishers.

Conzemius, A., & O'Neill, J. (2005). *The power of SMART goals: Using goals to improve student learning*. Bloomington, IN: Solution Tree Press.

Deal, T. E., & Kennedy, A. A. (2000). *Corporate cultures: The rites and rituals of corporate life*. New York, NY: Perseus Publishing.

Doran, G. T. (1981). There's a S.M.A.R.T. way to write management's goals and objectives. *Management Review*, *70*(11), 35.

Drach-Zahavy, A., & Erez, M. (2002). Challenge versus threat effects on the goal-performance relationship. *Organizational Behavior and Human Decision Process*, *88*(2), 667–682.

Duhigg, C. (2012). *The power of habit: Why we do what we do in life and business*. New York, NY: Random House.

Dunn, W. W. (2000). Habit: What's the brain got to do with it? *Occupational Therapy Journal of Research*, *20*(4S), 6S–20S.

Ehn, B., & Lofgren, O. (2009). Routines – made and unmade. In E. Shove, F. Trentmann, & R. Wilk (Eds.), *Time, consumption, and everyday life: Practice, materiality and culture* (pp. 99–112). London, UK: Bloomsbury Academic.

Fairweather, J. S. (2000). Diversification or homogenization: How markets and governments combine to shape American higher education. *Higher Education Policy*, *13*(1), 79–98.

Fairweather, J. S. (2002). The mythologies of faculty productivity: Implications for institutional policy and decision making. *Journal of Higher Education*, *73*(1), 26–48.

Finkelstein, M. J., Conley, V. M., & Schuster, J. H. (2016). *The faculty factor: Reassessing the American academy in a turbulent era*. Baltimore, MD: Johns Hopkins University Press.

51

Gallo, C. (2016). *The innovation secrets of Steve Jobs: Insanely different principles for breakthrough success*. New York, NY: McGraw-Hill.

Gappa, J. M., Austin, A. F., & Trice, A. G. (2007). *Rethinking faculty work: Higher education's strategic imperative*. San Francisco, CA: Jossey-Bass.

Gardner, S. K., & Veliz, D. (2014). Evincing the ratchet: A thematic analysis of the promotion and tenure guidelines at a striving university. *Review of Higher Education, 38*(1), 105–132.

Goleman, D. (2013). *Focus: The hidden driver of excellence*. New York, NY: HarperCollins Publishers.

Graybiel, A. M. (2008). Habits, rituals, and the evaluative brain. *Annual Review of Neuroscience, 31*, 359–387.

Harackiewicz, J. M., Barron, K. E., Tauer, J. M., & Elliot, A. J. (2002). Predicting success in college: A longitudinal study of achievement goals and ability measures as predictors of interest and performance from freshman year through graduation. *Journal of Educational Psychology, 94*(3), 562–575.

Harris, M. S., & Holley, K. A. (2016). Universities as anchor institutions: Economic and social potential for urban development. In M. B. Paulsen (Ed.), *Higher education: Handbook of theory and research* (pp. 393–440). Dordrecht, NL: Springer.

Harrison, B. J. (1999). Are you destined to burn out? *Fund Raising Management, 30*(3), 25–27.

Hart, J. L., & Cress, C. M. (2008). Are women faculty just "worrywarts?" Accounting for gender differences in self-reported stress. *Journal of Human Behavior in the Social Environment, 17*(1–2), 175–193.

Heath, C., & Heath, D. (2010). *Switch: How to change things when change is hard*. New York, NY: Crown Publishing.

Jacobs, J. A. (2004). Presidential addess: The faculty-time divide. *Sociological Forum, 19*(1), 3–27.

Jones, J. B. (2011). Expecting balance. *The Chronicle of Education*. Retrieved from www.chronicle.com/blogs/profhacker/expecting-balance/33675

Kahneman, D. (2013). *Thinking, fast and slow*. New York, NY: Farrar, Straus, and Giroux.

Kerr, S., & Landauer, S. (2004). Using stretch goals to promote organizational effectiveness and personal growth: General Electric and Goldman Sachs. *The Academy of Management Executive, 18*(4), 134–138.

Kerr, S., & LePelley, D. (2013). Stretch goals: Risks, possibilities, and best practices. In E. A. Locke & G. P. Lahtam (Eds.), *New developments in goal setting and task performance* (pp. 21–32). New York, NY: Routledge.

Kyvik, S. (2013a). The academic researcher role: Enhancing expectations and improved performance. *Higher Education, 65*(4), 525–538.

Kyvik, S. (2013b). Academic workload and working time: Retrospective perceptions versus time-series data. *Higher Education Quarterly, 67*(1), 2–14.

Lackritz, J. R. (2004). Exploring burnout among university faculty: Incidence, performance, and demographic issues. *Teaching and Teacher Education, 20*(7), 713–729.

Latham, G. P., & Locke, E. A. (2007). New developments in and directions for goal-setting research. *European Psychologist, 12*(4), 290–300.

Layzell, D. T. (1996). Faculty workload and productivity: Recurrent issues with new imperatives. *Review of Higher Education, 19*(3), 267–282.

Locke, E. A., & Latham, G. P. (1990). *A theory of goal setting and task performance.* Englewood Cliffs, NJ: Prentice-Hall.

McKeown, G. (2014). *Essentialism: The disciplined pursuit of less.* New York, NY: Crown Business.

Massy, W. F., & Zemsky, R. (1994). Faculty discretionary time: Departments and the "academic ratchet". *Journal of Higher Education, 65*(1), 1–22.

Menges, J. R. A. (1999). *Faculty in new jobs: A guide to settling in, becoming established, and building institutional support.* San Francisco, CA: Jossey-Bass.

Newport, C. (2016). *Deep work: Rules for focused success in a distracted world.* New York, NY: Grand Central Publishing.

Newton, T. (1999). Stress discourse and individualization. In C. Feltham (Ed.), *Controversies in psychotherapy and counseling* (pp. 241–251). London, UK: SAGE Publications.

Norcross, J. C., Mrykalo, M. S., & Blagys, M. D. (2002). Auld lang syne: Success predictors, change processes, and self-reported outcomes of New Year's resolvers and nonresolvers. *Journal of Clinical Psychology, 58*(4), 397–405.

Ophir, E., Nass, C., & Wagner, A. D. (2009). Cognitive control in media multitaskers. *Proceedings of the National Academy of Sciences of the United States of America, 106*(37), 15583–15587.

Perlow, L. A. (1999). The time famine: Towards a sociology of work. *Administrative Science Quarterly, 44*(1), 57–81.

Pink, D. H. (2005). *A whole new mind: Moving from the information age to the conceptual age.* New York, NY: Riverhead Books.

Plater, W. M. (1995). Future work faculty time in the 21st century. *Change: The Magazine of Higher Learning, 27*(3), 22–33.

Rhoades, G. (2009). From the general secretary: What we do to our young. *Academe, 95*(3). Retrieved from: www.aaup.org/AssociationofAmericanUniversityPresses/pubsres/academe/2009/MJ/col/ftgs.htm

Rice, R. E., Sorcinelli, M. D., & Austin, A. E. (2000). *Heeding new voices: Academic careers for a new generation.* Washington, DC: American Association for Higher Education.

Schuster, J. H., & Finkelstein, M. J. (2008). *The American faculty: The restructuring of academic work and careers.* Baltimore, MD: Johns Hopkins University Press.

Shahin, A., & Mahbod, M. A. (2007). Prioritization of key performance indicators: An integration of analytical hierarchy process and goal setting. *International Journal of Productivity and Performance Management, 56*(3), 226–240.

53

Tierney, W. G., & Bensimon, E. M. (1996). *Promotion and tenure: Community and socialization in academe*. Albany, NY: State University of New York Press.

Toutkoushian, R. K., & Bellas, M. L. (1999). Faculty time allocations and research productivity: Gender, race and family effects. *Review of Higher Education, 22*(4), 367–390.

Trower, C. A. (2012). *Success on the tenure track: Five keys to faculty job satisfaction*. Baltimore, MD: Johns Hopkins University Press.

Wolf-Wendel, L., & Ward, K. (2006). Faculty life at comprehensive universities: Between a rock and a hard place. *Journal of the Professoriate, 1*(2), 1–21.

Zemsky, R., Wegner, G. R., & Massy, W. F. (2005). *Remaking the American university: Market-smart and mission-centered*. New Brunswick, NJ: Rutgers University Press.

Ziker, J. P. (2014). The long, lonely road of homo academicus: Focusing the research lens on the professor's own schedule. *Blue Review*. Retrieved from: http://thebluereview. org/faculty-time-allocation/

Part II

Planning Your Route

Chapter 3

Scholarship and Academic Publishing

Publish or perish. Perhaps no other phrase in higher education describes as succinctly the reality and anxiety associated with obtaining tenure. While tenure policies and review committees certainly value other aspects of faculty work, the fact remains that at many institutions you must publish to get tenure. As the famous novelist Stephen King said in his wonderful tome, *On Writing: A Memoir of the Craft*, "Amateurs sit and wait for inspiration, the rest of us just get up and go to work" (King, 2010). And while expectations for research may differ from institution to institution, many universities expect, and require, substantial scholarship and publication. Publishing may look different across various disciplines—and even quite different within disciplines, such as the arts, that hold broader definitions of creative activity. In many cases, however, academic publishing represents the single most important factor in receiving tenure. Even in institutions that heavily emphasize teaching, publishing remains a significant factor in the tenure decision. This expectation means that pre-tenure faculty should spend a sizable amount of time, effort, and energy maximizing publication efforts.

Understanding the expectations for publishing in your department, institution, and discipline is essential. In many ways, the publication record separates easy from difficult decisions when a faculty member's tenure case comes up for a vote. Faculty who have worked hard on scholarship and maintained their productivity output present relatively simple decisions for external reviewers and tenure review committees. I suspect that most pre-tenure faculty understand at a basic level the necessity of academic publishing. The difficulty of even landing a tenure-track job today means most candidates can boast the CV and socialization to succeed in scholarship and academic publishing. Not only have you shown the ability to conduct this work in your graduate program and with your dissertation, but you are also likely to have published and presented several times in order to catch the eye of your hiring committee. Now, your challenge is prioritizing publishing—keeping it at the top of your to-do list and as a major focus during your pre-tenure years. This challenge may be the most significant one you face.

We would have a hard time finding an assistant professor who disagreed publishing was important. Yet, we could easily find someone whose failure to publish damaged their tenure case.

Moreover, publishing requires putting in the work during the first few years on the tenure track. Without the early spadework of data collection and analysis, you may end up with no results to publish. Moreover, journal review timelines are such that you simply cannot wait until your last year before going up for tenure in hopes of resurrecting your research productivity. In addition to this timeline consideration, you must remember that scholarship and publishing are activities, one of few in fact, where your tenure committees evaluate the regularity of your work. Case in point: If you start out with lower teaching evaluations and they get higher over time, the committee will give you credit for working to improve your teaching. But if you start out with a slow publication track record that escalates just before you go up for tenure, the committee may view this unfavorably, as a lack of seriousness regarding your research, and they may believe you are simply scrambling to salvage your tenure case.

All this to say, from day one, you need to keep publication at the heart of your work as a faculty member. Note that I did *not* say scholarship needs to *be* the heart of the work. I would guess intellectual curiosity and a love of scholarship drew many assistant professors to graduate school and, ultimately, to faculty life. In fact, these traits will help lead to a successful academic career. However, if you cannot translate scholarship into results—namely peer-reviewed, published manuscripts—your tenure case will suffer, perhaps fatally.

We can all debate whether the focus—hyper-focus, perhaps—on publication outputs benefits higher education. Many valid arguments suggest that the "publish or perish" mantra produces mediocre work and a glut of research (Altbach, 2013). I am sympathetic to many of these arguments, and I believe higher education should critically self-evaluate its expectations for publishing. We should debate the problematic measures of impact factors (Moed, 2010), the use of alternative metrics to evaluate scholarship (O'Meara, 2010), the potential and power of other publication venues such as blogs or social media (Gruzd, Staves, & Wilk, 2011), and the advantages and weaknesses of publication outlets such as open access journals (Creaser, 2010; Reinsfelder, 2012; Schroter & Tite, 2006). However, until these debates conclude with a general consensus among those faculty who will evaluate your tenure case, including external reviewers and those at your institution, you risk your tenure case by not playing the rules of the game as they are today. After successfully receiving tenure, I encourage faculty to jump wholeheartedly into these debates. But if you are unable to secure tenure first, you will not have a chance to change the long-term direction of the department, university, or discipline. You do not have to *like* the rules of the game, but you must understand them to set yourself up for success.

The bottom line is that publishing plays a vital role in a successful tenure case at many colleges and universities. These expectations differ across institutions and even across departments within institutions. However, some broad parameters can guide research activities during the pre-tenure years. In this chapter, I will address the ways scholarship and academic publishing are considered and evaluated, the decisions you must make to guide your research endeavors, and strategies and approaches the literature suggests can improve publication efforts. Taken together, your goal is to establish a scholarship and publication record in a way that you will not only find intellectually and personally fulfilling, but in way that also exceeds the threshold to satisfy the research expectations for tenure and promotion in your department, institution, and discipline.

TYPES OF ACADEMIC PUBLISHING

While publishing plays a critical role in building a successful case for tenure, unfortunately the criteria for academic publishing are more opaque than any other aspect of the tenure case. Institutions and tenure committees often prefer delineating vague policies to avoid putting hard and fast rules on academic publishing, in part, due to the wide variety of publishing outlets (Bentley & Kyvik, 2011; Harley & Acord, 2011). Committees may sidestep setting a requisite number of publications and refuse to rank publication outlets because this limits their flexibility to systematically review a tenure case. However, you should not confuse a lack of specific numbers with a lack of interest in impact factors, journal quality, and other similar metrics. Your committee might feel strongly about these metrics, even if they do not publicize a standard. The challenge for pre-tenure faculty rests in how to make sense of the high-stakes world of academic publishing with, at best, vague guidelines, or, at worst, no guidelines at all. What matters? How does the quality of one type of publication compare to another? Are conference proceedings considered prestigious publications or not considered at all? All of these questions, and many more, are context specific depending on your department, institution, and discipline. The growing number of open access and online journals—not to mention blogs, social media, and other online publications—only further complicates academic publishing today.

Each discipline sets different academic publishing expectations for prospective tenure candidates. In some disciplines, a book publication is required to success-fully receive tenure; in others, journal articles may prove the primary currency. While the value placed on various publication outlets varies by discipline, nine general types of academic publications exist as possible outlets for your scholarship. Pre-tenure faculty should consult with senior colleagues, mentors, and others in their particular field to determine how much attention to give to each type of publication. Here, I describe the range and array of options to help guide discussions about those most appropriate to your field of study.

59

Books and Monographs

Books and monographs explore a scholarly topic in long form format. Most books treat the subject under examination broadly, while monographs tend to focus in more detail on a specialized topic or aspect of the broader question. The necessity of publishing books or monographs varies dramatically among disciplines, with humanities and social science disciplines tending to rely on this publication type most frequently. However, even in disciplines that do not require book publishing, it can nevertheless be considered a significant accomplishment and evidence of major research contributions to the field. An exception to this category is textbooks, which may receive less weight at high research universities. Some tenure committees conceive of textbooks more as teaching than research, while others may argue that textbooks represent a lesser intellectual and scholarly contribution. The wide range in quality and type of books presents a challenge to evaluating their role in gaining tenure and promotion. In most cases, tenure committees evaluate books and monographs by considering the overall quality of the manuscript, data, arguments, quality and stature of the publisher (major university presses are considered most prestigious), book reviews, and citation evidence.

Edited Book

This type of book is an edited compilation of chapters around a central theme or subject from different authors. The editor collects the chapters, edits them, and works with the press. Edited books can be quite time intensive for editors, particularly if the quality of individual chapters proves lacking. Tenure committees often evaluate edited books based on the quality of the press, quality of the chapters, and the stature of the contributing authors. Generally speaking, an edited book would not receive the same weight and consideration as a regular book, assuming similar criteria such as the quality of the publisher or citation counts.

Journal Article

Journal articles are manuscripts that disseminate the findings of scholarly works published as part of a regular periodical. Journals may be called peer-reviewed journals, scholarly journals, academic journals, or other similar terms. Journal articles, as the backbone of academic publishing, will likely feature heavily in your case for tenure. Articles in scholarly journals are typically evaluated by some combination of the following criteria: peer-review status, impact factors, acceptance rates, stature of the editor or editorial board members, and the number of times the article has been cited.

Book Chapters

A book chapter is simply a chapter that appears as part of a larger volume. Typically, each chapter is written by a different group of authors. Two of the most common types of book chapters are edited and refereed. Edited book chapters are collected as part of an edited book and are reviewed by an editor. These chapters are rarely considered to be peer-reviewed. Refereed book chapters appear as handbooks (i.e., a research handbook) and have been peer-reviewed (sometimes by blind reviewers, sometimes not). Book chapters are typically evaluated on the quality of the manuscript, quality of the academic press, peer-review status, stature of the editor, and citation record of the chapter.

Book Reviews

Book reviews are short evaluations of a book providing an overview as well as a critical discussion of its content, style, and rigor. This publication type allows authors to analyze and react to the book as well as make recommendations to future readers. Even though book reviews are typically published in journals, they are rarely peer-reviewed or given significant weight in tenure decisions.

Conference Proceedings

This publication type constitutes a collection of papers presented at a professional association, meeting, symposium, or similar gathering. Conference proceedings are more common in the sciences and engineering fields, although even in these fields their prominence is diminishing (Larsen & Von, 2010). While some fields and disciplines consider proceedings to be evidence of significant research output, more often they receive little weight in a tenure review.

Reports

Reports include technical reports, scientific reports, and white papers. This fairly broad category includes a wide range of manuscripts describing the process or results of research or considering the current state of a research problem. Reports of this type rarely undergo peer review and are typically commissioned by an organization or agency. No real standards or streamlined procedures dictate the creation of these reports, which results in a great variety of products—even among reports examining similar issues. Most tenure committees consider reports unimportant to tenure decisions. To the extent that they are included as evidence of scholarship (and you may be able to make a compelling case, depending on the particulars of your situation), the impact of the report, stature of co-authors and the originating organization, and overall quality of the report can determine the level of the report's contribution to the scholarly and professional community.

Blogs and Online Writing

Despite their growing prominence and readership, blogs and other forms of online writing are valued less in the tenure process. For some disciplines, of course, individual circumstances might create an exception to this rule; however, the vast majority of online writing will not be considered part of the research portfolio for tenure promotion. At best, blogs and online writing are considered non-peer-reviewed publications. At worst (and quite likely), they are little valued and could even lead to questions as to why a candidate would publish in these outlets rather than in more traditional forums.

Op-Eds, Columns, and Publications for the Public

The last type of publication to consider is not really academic, per se, but constitute instead a forum for sharing scholarly expertise with the broader public. This type of publishing might include an op-ed in a local newspaper or a short piece in a magazine. Overall, this publication type includes any writing for the public sharing the results of research or scholarly understanding. Although tenure committees may not give this writing much value on the surface, writing for the public can effectively share your expertise outside of traditional academic publishing. Faculty committees will not typically assign much weight to this writing, but administrators may appreciate faculty who share their research outside of academe and receive press coverage for the institution.

PAUSE AND REFLECT

What are the major publication types in your field or discipline? Write down the most important publications for your tenure journey.

_____

_____

_____

_____

USE BACKWARD DESIGN TO PLAN YOUR RESEARCH

Once you understand the research expectations and merit of various publication outlets for tenure at your institution, you can begin to use backward design to plan your publications. Rooted in teaching theory, backward design approaches curriculum development by first creating learning goals (the "end product"), then working backward from those goals to determine instructional methods and assessments (Davidovitch, 2013; Richards, 2013). Backward design encourages teaching with specific goals in mind, which helps to focus and organize a course. In teaching, the backward design method provides a roadmap to guide the instructor; for other aspects of faculty life, however, this approach can also prove useful. In particular, backward designing your academic publication output can help provide a roadmap for your publishing activities.

Here is an example to illustrate this principle: In conversations with mentors and colleagues, a tenure candidate determines she needs 10 published or in-press articles prior to going up for tenure. On a typical timeline of going up for tenure at the beginning of her 6th year, this means publishing roughly two articles per year. This roadmap (see Figure 3.1) gives her a *rudimentary* guide. However, she knows that if she submits something in the spring of her fifth year, the publication may not get accepted before the beginning of her sixth year. Therefore, somewhere along the way, she adds a third publication during one of the early years to make up for the potential review time of a later publication. She can use this same backward process for each of the research publication expectations for tenure, including producing top-tier journal articles, book proposals, and conference proceedings.

As long as you can determine a reasonable goal before going up for tenure, you can formulate a timeline for what is needed each year to stay on track. You can even utilize this method with a specific manuscript. If your goal is to submit by Spring Break, you can work backward from that goal to set monthly, weekly, or daily tasks to complete the project on time.

Common tenure advice often incorporates the principles of backward design even if they are not defined as such. As an illustration, within the social sciences you may have heard the 2–2–2 advice for research productivity. That is, at any given time you should have two articles under review, two in the writing stage,

Year:	6th year	5th year	4th year	3rd year	2nd year	1st year
Number of articles under review		1	2	2	2	3
Number of publications by year		2	2	2	3	1
Cumulative publications	10	10	9	6	4	1

FIGURE 3.1 Publication Roadmap using Backward Design

WORKSHEET 3.1 BACKWARDS DESIGN ROADMAP

Step 1. Determine your publication goal.

How many publications do you need for tenure? Ex. 10 journal articles or 2 books.

_____

_____

_____

_____

Step 2. Determine the time available to complete the publication goal from Step 1.

When does your dossier need to be compiled for submission? How much time remains before this submission date?

_____

_____

_____

_____

Step 3. Create a roadmap (See Figure 3.1 for an example) for completing publications in allotted time.

Time:						
Number of articles under review						
Number of publications by year						
Cumulative publications						

and two at the data collection/analysis stage. While slightly different versions of this advice exist, the basic premise means you always have research at different stages of completion. As a result, you are able to show sustained effort (important for tenure) while also meeting the quantitative publication expectations at your institution. Other colleges or universities may necessitate more of a 1–1–1 or even a 3–3–3. The primary point here suggests that pre-tenure faculty have publications at various stages and produce enough manuscripts to meet or exceed the research expectations of tenure. Backward design presents the best process by which to spell out intermediate goals and build sufficient research activity and a tenure-worthy CV, rather than working haphazardly toward an unspecified end goal.

DEVELOPING A RESEARCH AGENDA

A tenure candidate's research agenda plays a critical part in designing scholarly and publication activities. Establishing your research agenda means deciding which research areas you will explore and the methodologies you will employ, then letting these guide your research activities. As we have all probably heard from our own graduate school professors, it is impossible to study everything in your field, and you must focus on topics that prove interesting to you and present solid publishing opportunities. Tenure committees generally like to see assistant professors establish a consistent line of research or a few complementary lines of research, comprising their research agenda. Because of this, you should avoid a scattershot approach to research by developing a clear agenda and following it in your scholarly activities.

There are several philosophical and practical reasons to establish your research agenda early in your career. First, universities want to see that you are working toward, or have achieved, a national reputation in your field of expertise. A tightly focused research agenda helps achieve this desired prominence through specialty in a specific area. If your research bounces around among a variety of relatively disconnected projects, it becomes difficult for your committee, and particularly external reviewers, to establish and validate your areas of expertise. Additionally, your work on multiple similar research studies creates significant efficiencies for you. For example, you do not need to learn a new body of research in order to write your literature reviews, and you are already familiar with journals that publish on your topic. Overall, if you maintain consistency with your topic, you can more easily and quickly publish your research.

Many early career faculty that I have worked with do not have a single line of inquiry forming their research agenda. Tenure committees and external reviewers understand this; they know that you may not have a single, isolated line of academic exploration. They realize that prospective candidates may have, for example, two related concepts that they studied extensively in graduate school, worked on as part of a laboratory, or which were part of their dissertation. As long as you can articulate each line of inquiry, describe the relationships between each line, and demonstrate your expertise in the two (or at most three) lines of academic inquiry, most review committees will find this appropriate. However, if your research appears to be a collection of random projects lacking a common thread, tenure committees may rightly question whether you have demonstrated expertise and developed the level of national reputation necessary to achieve tenure.

For pre-tenure faculty struggling to articulate their own research agendas, I recommend studying the careers of major researchers in your field. To do this, get a copy of the vita of a significant and well-respected researcher. Next, look at the years prior to when this established scholar received tenure—you will see how their line of research progressed throughout their career. In academic research, it takes a while to build up the knowledge and data to answer specific questions. Over time, as an academic's methodologies advance and their knowledge base grows, you will likely see their research questions change. When looking at a full professor with 25 years of research experience, for example, many pre-tenure faculty fail to fully appreciate how research agendas evolve. These professors did not magically exit graduate school with the focus and expertise they possess today. By studying the early years of prominent researchers, you can learn how their agendas evolved and grew over time, which can help you compose your own research agenda.

In addition, examining the research agenda of a senior colleague in your field can help show how they bring disparate ideas together. Think about it: There are many ideas that may seem inseparable today, but this may not have been the case at the early part of the expert's career. When studying a senior professor's research agenda, you can begin to see the connections and the concepts that anchor an entire research career. While the context, the theoretical framing, and methodological approaches may be different throughout the years, the common underlying themes that form the foundation of their research agenda will become apparent. Pre-tenure faculty should take time to delineate these central concepts in their own work early in their careers, working to both articulate and foreground them in the research they will undertake during the pre-tenure years.

Just as a meeting agenda provides a list of decision points for discussion, a research agenda provides a framework for making decisions about research activities. During the first few years as a faculty member, it is tempting to jump at any research opportunity that comes along. When you are worried about having a significant number of publications, any potential promise of publication looks attractive. You will need a lens through which to determine whether to pursue any given opportunity. A strong and clearly articulated research agenda can serve this purpose, providing boundaries for scholarly activities and publishing. New projects and initiatives may easily capture your attention, but evaluating a new research opportunity's relationship to the research agenda will help you better consider the worthiness of a project. Only if a new opportunity is in line with your research agenda should you then ask more nuanced questions such as the amount of time it requires or its value to tenure review committees. Even if the opportunity provides access to the top journal in your field or to a prestigious conference, I would recommend thinking twice and discussing with mentors before pursuing a publication not in line with your research agenda. Establishing a research agenda and sharing it with colleagues lays the groundwork for all the research activities you will undertake during your pre-tenure years.

EXTERNAL GRANTS AND CONTRACTS

The availability of, and expectations for, grant and contract funding can vary tremendously across institutions and disciplines. In some departments, a successful research agenda and tenure case requires grant and contract funding for basic support, while in other departments, external funding is not required. In part, this difference derives from the disparity in available funding by discipline. While grants may not be required in your department, all universities love to see faculty receive external funding of some kind. I strongly urge pre-tenure faculty to figure out early on, preferably during the hiring process, the university's grant funding expectations at the departmental, school, and institutional level. Grants might be required, helpful but not required, or not highly valued depending on the particular situation, and this is good to know in advance. Although pre-tenure faculty are unlikely to find written requirements for how much external support they need to receive in funding-required situations, candidates nevertheless should try to discern the unwritten or unofficial expectations from the dean, department chair, and senior colleagues. If no one is able to provide a good estimate, consult with recently tenured candidates to get some idea of what has been sufficient in recent cases.

In disciplines with limited grant opportunities, faculty may find themselves particularly challenged by the amount of time required to write grant and contract proposals. This is because of the way we are used to writing. If you write a journal article of reasonable quality, you will likely find a publication outlet of some kind for your work; in contrast, most of the grant applications that you write will get rejected. There is a silver lining, however: You do not need to receive that many grants to meet external funding expectations, even in departments requiring grant funding. I suspect that, if every 2–3 years you receive a grant of reasonable size ("reasonable" will be determined by your department and research agenda), you will have sufficient resources for your work and meet the expectations of your tenure committee.

When considering "reasonable" funding in a particular situation, think about the degree to which your research agenda requires grant funding to operate.

If you need resources to fund laboratory expenses, for example, you will obviously need to secure funding just to support your basic research endeavors. Moreover, you should consider the amount of money the university spent to bring you to campus in start-up costs, laboratory renovations, or equipment purchases. Hopefully, no dean or department chair would describe a tenure case quite so bluntly, but it is true that candidates must consider, to an extent, how they will repay the institution for its investment in their research program. A dean who puts up $200,000 to help establish a lab may be less than thrilled if a pre-tenure faculty's research does not bring in any external support.

Research grants are beneficial for faculty even in those disciplines where scholarship does not require funding for basic operations and support. Ultimately, grant funding enables you to do more and extend your work beyond what you can accomplish without external funding. Grants and contracts assist with bringing students in on research projects, which can improve the efficiency and speed of research. Funding can substantially expand the scope and scale of your scholarly activities. In addition to supporting students and other initiatives that can improve scholarship, funding helps take research activities to another level. Although varying by discipline, funding may help add research sites, collect or access more data, put research into practice in professional or real-world settings, or enable "buying out" of teaching to focus more on scholarship and other opportunities.

In order for you to successfully pursue external grants and contracts, some small and relatively simple tasks can be useful. First, ask colleagues and mentors for examples of successful grant applications, particularly for agencies and foundations that may support your research work. Grant writing differs from publishing scholarly articles, so seeking exemplars can help you understand what a successful proposal entails. Additionally, serving as a reviewer on panels for grants in the field can help you see the review process and learn about successful and unsuccessful proposals. Obviously, you should only do this review activity in moderation; nevertheless, the process can prove beneficial for learning more about funding in your field.

Many universities offer internal grant competitions to help assistant professors develop a history of funding. These internal grants are often open to all pre-tenure faculty across campus—even those in disciplines with limited external funding potential. If you are in one of these disciplines, such as the humanities, internal grants can not only support scholarship, but can also show small grant activity in the tenure file. In addition, internal grants prove useful for collecting pilot data that can justify support for larger external grants.

Building from an internal grant competition, you may begin seeking small external grants to support research. If necessary, start with small grants from internal and external sources. Working on projects with senior colleagues can also develop experience working on grants. Once you build up a track record of funding, you can grow to medium-sized and larger grants. While you may not land the huge grant right away (as some funders need evidence of a history of successful projects), often you can leverage smaller successes into larger ones.

As with many research related decisions, you must consider many pros and cons when it comes to external funding, with no clear right or wrong choices in many situations. Given the limited amount of time to publish during the pre-tenure years, some faculty, particularly in those fields that do not require grants, worry about devoting themselves to grants when the potential payoff is so much less certain than with journal articles. This is a reasonable concern, and one that justifies giving serious thought to planning research activities. If you decide to pursue funding, I strongly encourage perseverance. As I noted earlier, many of your proposals will likely be rejected. The National Institutes for Health rejects 80 percent of grant applications (National Institutes of Health, 2017) while the National Science Foundation rejects 76 percent of proposals (National Science Foundation, 2016). Take the feedback from reviewers, address criticisms, and re-apply. Many successful grants require two or three attempts before successfully securing funding. Because the potential of not being funded is so high, I advise you to make the most out of your grant proposals. Avoid wasted effort during the limited time available for research prior to going up for tenure. One way to do this with grant proposals is to reuse the text for journal articles. For example, the background section of a grant proposal could serve as a publishable literature review or summary article. While the grant may or may not receive funding, the time you spend on the proposal will not be wasted because the foundational text can form a possible publication in the future. In the end, grants and contracts can play a critical role in a successful tenure case, but pre-tenure faculty should think strategically before pursuing them.

ACADEMIC CONFERENCES AND MEETINGS

Depending on your perspective, professional travel and presenting at conferences can be an enjoyable or tedious aspect of faculty work. You may have valid reasons to limit your professional travel, from health concerns to family obligations. Faculty who are single parents or adult caretakers may find travel difficult to arrange. Moreover, universities may pay for your direct travel expenses, but not for additional expenses such as childcare or pet boarding (Dean & Koster, 2014). Many faculty absorb at least some professional travel expenses beyond what their universities reimburse.

In addition, many institutions have restricted the funding they provide for faculty travel due to declining state support for higher education and general tightening of university expenses around the country (Hossler, Lund, Westfall, & Irish, 1997; Tandberg, 2010; Zusman, 2005). As a result, you may have to decide between conferences your university will fund and those you will need to fund yourself. Be creative about finding sources of funding from a variety of internal and external sources. In the end, if you are forced to decide how many conferences you can attend, for personal or financial reasons, I would encourage you to determine how many times you are able to travel and then identify the best opportunities to advance your tenure case.

The greatest advantage of conferences and, more broadly, speaking engagements at other institutions is networking. Your institution likely values, at least to some degree, your national reputation in your area of study. As a result, you need to gain attention for your research. Publishing alone often proves insufficient to develop a national reputation in your area. You need to interact with people and share your scholarly work in order to establish your reputation. While invited talks are a great way to do this, conferences prove one of the easiest and most efficient ways to achieve this goal.

Academic conferences and meetings offer many opportunities to engage with your field, from formal research sessions where you share your work to informal receptions or hallway conversations. But while these types of interactions can critically support your scholarship, many faculty find the thought of schmoozing at conferences anxiety inducing. I suspect this occurs, at least in part, because strong personalities dominate face-to-face interactions (Anderson & Kilduff, 2009). I am sympathetic. I despise small talk, networking, and some of the seemingly forced interactions that often happen at conferences. And I am not alone in this; Susan Cain left her career in corporate law for similar reasons. Cain's popular book, *Quiet: The Power of Introverts in a World that Can't Stop Talking*, examines these exact struggles. Her research drives home the idea that "there's zero correlation between the gift of gab and good ideas," despite the seeming advantage of extroversion (Cain, 2013, p. 5).

Even for those of us who feel ill at ease networking, there are other ways to engage with fellow scholars and build the connections necessary for establishing our reputations in the field. For example, I have always felt more comfortable taking on service opportunities that provide a more formal way to get to know other scholars. I find that, on a committee for an academic professional organization, the assignments and structures reduce my reservations about meeting new people. When I have a role and assigned task, I can make genuine connections without being forced into dreaded small talk over cheap wine at a conference reception in a hotel lobby.

Networking and conference attendance not only get your name and research out into the field, but conferences can also help your scholarship in other ways. Conferences offer occasions to find partners for collaboration on future research projects. Unless you are in an exceptionally large area of research, you know, or will soon discover, the relatively small number of people who do work in areas similar to yours. I encourage you to build and develop relationships with fellow researchers, as these collaborations can be a boon to your research activities. You can find future co-authors, potential sources of new data, or peers with whom to share ideas about your research. The odds are that few colleagues at your home institution have exactly the same research agenda as you. Otherwise, why would you have been hired? As a result, identifying colleagues at other institutions can benefit your scholarly activities for the rest of your career.

In addition, conferences enable you to reach out to senior colleagues who do research similar to your own. A good challenge is to schedule at least one of these meetings at every conference you attend. I suspect you will find senior scholars are generally open to meeting early career scholars doing similar research to their own. Occasionally, of course, you may run into someone unapproachable, who ignores your email, or who legitimately does not have time to meet with you. However, I think you will find that you can most often schedule these types of meetings, and that most senior scholars are interested in discussing their research with you. In order to set up meetings, you should schedule prior to the conference. Scheduling meetings once you arrive at a conference presents a host of logistical challenges, meaning the best chance of arranging a meeting is prior to the start of the conference.

Scholarship, by its nature, requires engagement with other researchers. From a basic level of peer review to external letters for tenure, the quality and value of your scholarship is, at least to some degree, determined by others in your field. In the end, one of the best ways to get your work out there and in front of other scholars is through academic conferences and meetings. As a result, conferences should be a significant priority during your pre-tenure years. Presenting at conferences will not substitute for the need to publish described at the beginning of this chapter, but the benefits of conferences are well worth the investment in time and energy.

WRITING COLLABORATIONS

Collaboration and co-authoring with colleagues at your current institution, at institutions around the country, or even globally offers a potentially stimulating opportunity for your research program. Working with another researcher or a team of researchers can add to the quality and quantity of your scholarship (Uddin, Hossain, Abbasi, & Rasmussen, 2012). Co-authors can bring skills to the table that you do not have, share the workload on a paper, and simply make a project more engaging than working in isolation. Another significant advantage of collaborators is the degree of accountability they often provide. While you may be okay missing your own personal writing deadline, you will likely think twice about missing a deadline for something you owe your co-author. In many fields of study, collaboration is the norm in academic publishing. I bet, in any field, if you look at the most productive scholars, you will find a series of collaborations that helped drive research activities.

Given all the benefits of collaboration (He, Geng, & Campbell-Hunt, 2009; Lee & Bozeman, 2005), there are a few things you should do before beginning a collaborative project to set yourself up for success. Ideally, you want to learn about a collaborator's work style and other commitments before joining a project. Nearly every faculty member has a story about a collaboration gone wrong because his or her co-author lacked work ethic or defined work differently, was overloaded, or was not committed to the project. While complementary work styles can be a tremendous benefit, someone who consistently misses deadlines or submits poor quality work can derail a research project more quickly than just about anything else.

Working with someone else obviously requires more coordination than working on a project alone. Actively managing the collaboration can ensure the project's success (Bammer, 2008). In most instances, the inefficiencies of holding meetings or conference calls to discuss a study are more than offset by the advantage of having more than one person completing research tasks (Cummings & Hass, 2012). However, be aware of collaborators who *discuss* research more than they *conduct* research. These unproductive collaborations, beyond failing to progress your study, additionally waste time that could be spent on manuscripts that are moving closer to submission. You can avoid these types of collaborations by delineating clear deadlines and agendas for research meetings. For example, if the purpose of a research meeting is to discuss your data analysis but the analysis has not yet been run, you do not need to have the meeting.

Technology makes it possible to collaborate with scholars from across the world. Videoconferences and file sharing through various cloud services have revolutionized research collaboration. Despite these advances, you should still find time to get together with your colleagues to work on your research project face-to-face (Sonnenwald, 2007). For colleagues on campus, this could be as simple as going for a cup of coffee to discuss next steps. In other cases, you might find time at a conference or schedule a campus visit. To maximize your progress during face-to-face meetings, especially with colleagues who live far away, prioritize the research work requiring the most significant amount of back and forth engagement. This could include coming up with the research plan or working through your approach to data analysis. Regular updates and draft sharing can be done easily via technology, but high engagement activities in person will save you a great deal of time and stave off the need for repetitive video calls or dozens of back and forth emails.

Of course, problems arise during research collaborations; often, collaborators disagree on author order and the division of work. Guidelines for author order can vary depending on your discipline (Creamer, 2004; Graf et al., 2007; Hundley, Van Teijlingen, & Simkhada, 2013). In some fields, author order is determined by the largest contribution to the manuscript, while in others authors may be listed alphabetically. In the social sciences, on the one hand, the first author is often the most significant contributor; in the sciences, on the other hand, the principal investigator is often listed last. Even with guidelines from your field, you need to clarify authorship and research responsibilities prior to beginning a new project. Who is taking the lead? What will be the authorship order? If the study develops into multiple papers, will we take turns with authorship? These decisions are much better dealt with at the planning phase of the project than at the end, when longstanding and unspoken differences of opinions can lead to awkward discussions. Failing to get everyone on the same page at the start of a project can sour relationships and even derail your research.

As with any good relationship, the best research collaborations develop trust and open communication. At some point, you will disagree with your co-author(s). If you deal with these disagreements through a healthy process, working through them can improve your study as you grapple with different scholarly viewpoints. Bridging such differences can be easier if you and your collaborator are of generally similar experience and rank. If your collaborator is more senior or junior than you, consider the collaboration's power dynamics and temper your responses appropriately (Shaikh, 2015). Of course, in many cases, there is no right or wrong step forward. Research often involves tradeoffs, and considering a disagreement from your colleague's perspective can help identify key areas to explore further. No matter who is right or wrong, discussing concerns with your colleague and building trust from the beginning can mitigate many research disputes. In the end, you do not want things to endanger your current and potentially future work. Finding good collaborators can be difficult, so try to work through your concerns with an eye toward maintaining strong connections—even if you decide not to pursue future research opportunities with this particular collaborator.

PAUSE AND REFLECT

List your current collaborators. Then, brainstorm a few potential collaborators for future projects.

_____

_____

_____

_____

Collaborating and Writing with Students

When considering collaboration, one group warrants special attention. Graduate and undergraduate students can be tremendously beneficial to your research endeavors, and they can embody a merger between your teaching and research activities. For all the benefits of working with students, however, there are concerns and challenges. With any type of student, but particularly doctoral students, you must essentially perform a consistent balancing act (Shaikh, 2015). Doctoral students are an important source of academic labor to further your work, particularly in laboratory-based disciplines. However, doctoral students are more than just grist for the tenure mill, so when you take on a doctoral student you must balance your research needs with their academic needs. Often, pre-tenure faculty worry about their own research activities—understandably—and fail to fully appreciate their responsibility to help students establish their own scholarly career (Rice, Sorcinelli, & Austin, 2000).

One of the biggest challenges as a new faculty member is transitioning from advisee to adviser. Hopefully, through the course of your graduate work, you took on greater roles in research projects and became somewhat accustomed to leading intellectually. If not, I strongly encourage you to work with trusted mentors to develop this skill in the early faculty years. You need to take ownership of not only the work of your projects but also its intellectual leadership. Developing the ability to guide projects as the lead researcher, rather than as a doctoral or post-doctoral member of the research team, presents one of the most significant differences between a faculty versus doctoral student role (Lovitts, 2005, 2008).

Beyond owning the leadership and mentoring role you now play, a few other considerations come up when working with students. First, authorship can prove touchy for early career faculty and doctoral students. Authorship is less of a concern in fields with standard norms for authorship order. But in those fields where authorship order indicates level of contribution, deciding author order with students presents a potential minefield. Unfortunately, there are no hard and fast rules to guide these decisions. You should consult with colleagues, mentors, and others to help decide author order on a case-by-case basis. Ultimately, as with all co-authorship relationships, you need to discuss contribution and authorship with your student collaborators at the beginning of the project. This ensures everyone is on the same page regarding expectations.

In terms of your tenure case, many institutions will look favorably on research conducted with students, regardless of whether they are at the undergraduate or graduate level. Working with students is often viewed as a sign of your mentorship ability and willingness, which can strongly support your case for tenure and promotion. I once had a senior colleague describe this type of work as receiving "bonus points," because everyone knows that co-authoring with a student consumes more time than co-authoring with a peer. Especially if you are in a field that values co-authorship with students, you may even want to note in some small way on your CV or in your tenure dossier that a specific publication marked a collaboration with students.

The expectations for research at your institution may impact how your tenure committees view student co-authorship. While not all institutions with higher teaching loads or lower expectations for research value working with students more, there are a couple of reasons why they often do. First, universities with lower research expectations often have larger numbers of students, particularly in professional fields such as education. In these institutions, faculty often carry higher teaching and advising loads; thus, they have more potential student collaborators. Second, research expectations at these types of institutions often include a broader acceptable array of publication outlets, making it easier to include student collaborators. If you work at one of these institutions or have senior colleagues who previously worked at an institution of this type, you will likely hear advice to publish frequently with students. You may be advised to help students publish from their dissertation work or take class papers and bring them up to publishable quality. If this type of publishing is recognized by your institution, you should consider taking it on. However, if your institution has high research expectations for tenure or would look poorly on a faculty member co-authoring an article based on an advisee's dissertation, you obviously want to avoid this kind of work. As with all advice related to tenure, you ultimately have to balance your career aspirations, tenure expectations at your institution, and the advice from a variety of colleagues and mentors.

I want to include a final note of caution about your research relationships with students, and it regards the inclusion of students as co-authors. In many instances, including a student on a research project is a no-brainer; in these cases, questions about authorship order or the level of intellectual contribution need to be addressed, but not questions regarding the student's inclusion. To be sure, if a student contributes intellectually, he or she should receive authorship credit and you should not take sole credit. This does not mean, however, that if a student provides *any* research assistance on a project that he or she automatically gets authorship credit. Again, know the norms in your field and seek guidance to make sure you are doing right by your students. But know that, while many tenure review committees view working with students favorably, there may be instances where excessive work with a student leads to questions concerning your independence. You never want your tenure review to raise questions of whether you are riding the coattails of your students. You may find that you have a colleague with strong opinions on this point or find yourself in a department with baggage on this issue, perhaps due to events that occurred before you even arrived at the institution. At the end of the day, you need to understand the norms around co-authoring with students and uncover any unwritten rules to evaluating whether, and to what extent, to co-author with students.

Working with students offers enormous benefits during your pre-tenure years. Not only can students supercharge your research activities, they can also provide the types of mentorship and teaching opportunities that led you to faculty work in the first place. For these reasons, I encourage you to work with students when doing so presents a win-win opportunity for you both. But be sure you go into work with students with a full understanding of the potential pitfalls of these relationships. Throughout my career, I have found these experiences among the most rewarding of all my faculty work, and I trust you will find them beneficial as well. To help ensure success though, take the time to think through potential problems, seek advice, and openly communicate, so that working with students can benefit your tenure case and faculty career.

DEVELOPING PRODUCTIVE WRITING PRACTICES

I suspect that nearly every pre-tenure professor, at some time or another, has heard the advice to write every day. This advice is ubiquitous in part because research shows it can profoundly improve your writing productivity as a new professor (Silvia, 2007). I remember hearing this advice during my first days as an assistant professor and being profoundly frustrated by it. Few things were as scary and frustrating to me as starting with a blank page. I could not imagine facing the power and potential of the blinking cursor every day. Of course, we all have a million reasons not to write. Every faculty member has faced one or more internal or external blocks on writing (Boice, 1993). Internal blocks include being demoralized from a particularly harsh review or having concerns about being an imposter. A cognitive distortion that prevents someone from feeling a sense of accomplishment from an achievement, imposter syndrome is alive and well among scholars (Gravois, 2007). Your goal should be to tame your inner gremlin (Carson, 2003), which thrives on fear and promotes procrastination, to limit your self-defeating behaviors and beliefs.

One of the best pieces of advice to help get over internal blocks and even just improve your writing generally is Anne Lamott's (1994) suggestion to write "shitty first drafts" (p. 21). A shitty first draft lets you just get words on the page without worrying about their quality or what your inner critic may say about them. Later, you can worry about editing and addressing any flaws. Attempting to get uncensored words out onto paper can help you make remarkable progress with your writing. Through the entire writing of the book you are now reading, I used the shitty first draft method. If you saw the original version of this chapter, for example, you would recognize some parts that have stayed largely the same, while other sections have been completely rewritten or cut from the final form.

In many ways, we academics have been ruined by our prior success in school. Odds are, if you are now a faculty member, you were a pretty good student; this is how you ended up in graduate school and with a faculty position. Unfortunately, the writing and study techniques many of us used to get through school fail us later in graduate school or when we start on the tenure track. I, for example, was a U.S. history major as an undergraduate at the University of North Carolina. As such, I was accustomed to generating history essays at the drop of a hat. In a few hours at best or an all-nighter at worse, I could create a history essay that would get a good grade. I would create one draft, spellcheck it (maybe), and submit it. The concept of writing in drafts, seeking feedback, and refining my ideas through writing was foreign to me. Through much of my coursework in graduate school, I continued using a similar process. I had to work harder and seek some feedback, but I generally could get by pretty well in my courses. On research projects I had other authors, particularly faculty advisers, to guide the process, so my research process was driven primarily by their work habits (for you, this may have been a good or bad experience depending on your luck with advisers). Often, as happened for me, when you go on the tenure track and begin to drive your own writing process, the poor writing habits of your undergraduate and graduate school days re-emerge.

In addition to internal blocks like imposter syndrome and procrastination, external blocks to writing may include other faculty responsibilities or a lack of writing time. Faculty face many external blocks that revolve around scheduling. A time management plan can help. Expert Stephen Covey (1990) popularized a time management matrix that can help you think about scheduling your writing. By considering the urgency and importance of your competing responsibilities, you can determine how to prioritize your writing time. Urgent are projects or tasks that have an encroaching, time-sensitive deadline. Important signifies that the project or task is substantial and meaningful for meeting your goals. Use Worksheet 3.2 to write down a few of your research priorities.

The Covey Time Management Quadrants:

- Quadrant I: Urgent & Important
  - Example: Completing journal article revisions by editor's deadline
- Quadrant II: Not Urgent & Important
  - Example: Analyzing data
- Quadrant III: Urgent & Not Important
  - Example: Ordering lab supplies
- Quadrant IV: Not Urgent & Not Important
  - Example: Skimming journals to see what is out there

If you are like most people, I suspect you spend much of your time in the "Urgent & Not Important" category. Much of the shallow work discussed in Chapter 2 falls into this category as the urgent drowns out the important. Your challenge is to reorient your daily and weekly schedule around accomplishing your most important work, which at many institutions means academic publishing. Many tactical approaches are out there to help with writing (Belcher, 2009; Hartley, 2008; Murray, 2013; Silvia, 2007). For starters, you should schedule

WORKSHEET 3.2 COVEY TIME MANAGEMENT GRID

	URGENT	NOT URGENT
IMPORTANT	Quadrant I: Urgent & Important	Quadrant II: Not Urgent & Important
NOT IMPORTANT	Quadrant III: Urgent & Not Important	Quadrant IV: Not Urgent & Not Important

Adapted from: Covey (1990)

writing appointments with yourself and treat these appointments like class: unmissable. Additionally, plan your writing sessions early in the day, if your teaching schedule permits, to avoid letting the urgent things that come up during the day distract you from your writing.

Many faculty face the challenge of finding large chunks of time for writing activities. In most faculty jobs, you will struggle to block massive amounts of time for anything. However, this is okay and even potentially advantageous for you. Large blocks of time can lead to binge writing, which is less effective and more counterproductive than daily writing (Silvia, 2007). In the best empirical examination of this claim, Robert Boice (1990) studied faculty who wrote in "brief daily sessions" versus those who wrote in large blocks of time. Faculty who wrote in daily sessions not only produced more (157 pages compared to 17 pages) but also ended up spending double the amount of time writing. Boice showed the benefits of working on writing, though what exactly this means can vary. If you have not written in months, for example, just spending 30 minutes a day can be a huge victory. If you write regularly, however, you might focus on stretching 1-hour sessions to 90 minutes. In many ways, the amount of time you spend writing proves less important than the principle of writing a bit multiple times a week, rather than in binge sessions right before a deadline. Personally, I find that 2 hours is a good amount of time for me to focus on writing. Depending on what I am writing and on my other obligations, I can sometimes stretch this closer to 4 hours. The few times when I have tried writing for more than 4 hours, I have become unproductive, gotten burned out, and have had a harder time getting back into writing the next day.

Binge writing results in a terribly unproductive cycle. For example, let's say you have procrastinated on a project until you are up against a hard deadline. You spend three straight days cranking out a manuscript of less than your best work, but you meet your deadline. After the three day binge session, you are fried and do not want to think of doing much work for a week or two. You find that other to-do list items backed up during your binging, and now you need to get those done. So, you take another week to work on those items. At this point, it has been three weeks since you completed any writing. You start feeling guilty and the thought of sitting down and writing generates great anxiety. After another week or two of anxiety, it has been five or six weeks since you did any writing, and now another deadline is approaching rapidly. You spend three days binge writing to get a serviceable draft completed. Rinse and repeat.

How to Actually Write Every Day

There is a better way. While you might be able to get tenure with binge writing, there are clearly better ways to get your writing goals accomplished. What I ultimately realized is that starting with the blank page is only one way of daily writing. I doubt many professors out there can sit down and tackle a blank page every single day. So how do you reconcile the advice to write every day with the inability to tackle the dreaded blinking cursor? You can use different types of writing to move a project forward, and you should consider each of these below for the purposes of daily writing.

Brain dump: In the spirit of Anne Lamott's (1994) shitty first draft, sometimes I just do a brain dump of everything I know or think about a topic. This type of writing focuses on getting ideas down on paper that you may later work into usable prose. For example, you might write more informally than you would in typical academic writing or leave notations to yourself for future editing. I use XXXX placeholders for where additional material will be added rather than stopping to look up the information and disrupt my writing flow. While many pieces may not get used in a later draft, this writing can serve as the bare bones draft for various sections of your manuscript.

Edit for content: This type of writing is useful when you already have a drafted manuscript. In this round of editing, you focus on substance, not style. Do you have all the main ideas? Are they clearly described? Do you provide examples to help your reader understand the points you are making? Your focus in editing for content is that you are clearly communicating your most important points to your reader.

Line editing: Next, you focus on the style and prose of your writing. Check your grammar and make sure that you followed all the appropriate conventions of writing. Trying to edit for substance and style simultaneously proves difficult if not impossible because you are looking for two different aspects of your writing. I strongly suggest that you separate the process of editing into two different rounds.

Restructure: After completing an early draft of your work, examine the structure to see if you clearly communicate your ideas. Move paragraphs as needed to improve the flow and logic of your manuscript.

Figures and tables: You should not stop in the middle of your writing to work on figures and tables. Rather, figures and tables should be undertaken when you need a little mental break from the challenge of creating new prose. Putting together figures and tables is important and necessary, and you should consider it as satisfying your daily writing requirement.

References: I highly encourage all new professors to use some type of bibliographic software, which saves a tremendous amount of time and energy. Yet, even with the assistance of software, you must allocate time for working on references. Similar to figures and tables, working on references offers another task to work on when you need a respite from the challenge of creating new text.

Blank page: At some point, you must put fingers to the keyboard and write. You cannot edit or add references if there is no text to work with in the first place. While the ideas listed above are all helpful to making progress on your daily writing, you must not lose sight of the need to get words on the page. Some days you just have to sit down and create.

Obviously, these aspects of writing are easier or harder depending on your personality and the demands of the day, so adjust what you do on a given day based on your schedule and your mental energy. And remember, writing takes many forms other than simply working with the blank page. If the blank page is all you think about, you are unlikely to write on a daily basis. Given the overwhelming evidence about the potential of working on your writing every day, I highly suggest that you prioritize accomplishing these different types of daily writing.

A Few Tips to Get Your Writing Groove Back

When I talk with graduate students or pre-tenure faculty, they often assume that senior scholars have some special experience or ability that makes them better writers. While experience and practice certainly helps, as the novelist J.A. Jance (2016, p. para. 9) once said, "a writer is someone who has written something today." Whether due to some internal or external writing block (Flaherty, 2005), we all lose our writing groove from time to time. The challenge is figuring out the strategies to employ to get back to writing productively. Fortunately, some relatively simple strategies suggest ways to reset writing and move past blocks (Boice, 1990, 1993).

Tip 1. Set a Goal For Your Writing

When you are getting back into writing, I suggest setting a goal based on time rather than on creating a certain number of words or pages. I often set a specific time period in which I will write along with a minimum word count. However, if I am struggling with writing, I will frequently only set a time goal of 1 hour. Typically, I can produce at least 750 words an hour; but if I am struggling, I do not worry about word count as much as spending the time. I know the words will eventually flow if I spend time writing. Whether your goal is time spent or a specific word count attained, the simple act of setting aside the time to write (and sticking to it) is more important at this stage. The desire to complete your goal that day can help overcome procrastination, revive your motivation, or refocus your priorities (Mehta, 2012; Renfree, Harrison, Marshall, Stawarz, & Cox, 2016).

Tip 2. Change Your Writing Location

I am always amazed at how well this works. All you have to do is go somewhere different and almost immediately the vibe changes. Going to a new coffee shop or finding a nice corner on campus can help get you going again. It really does not matter where you go as long as the spot is somewhere different from your usual writing location.

Tip 3. Write About Something Different

Particularly if you are stuck because a major writing project is looming, take some time to write about something else. While this advice may seem counterintuitive, one of the best things you can do is get words on a page and exercise your writing muscles. Maybe you have a conference proposal to work on or a book review that you are writing. It really does not matter what you write— just get writing! As you begin re-engaging your writing muscles, you will find yourself in a better place with your writing, and you will be ready to tackle your big project in a day or two after you have regained your writing mojo.

Tip 4. Find a Template or Example

When you have a template or example to use, you can more easily imagine what your writing projects will look like when completed. A template assists with visualizing the end and what you need to get there. Moreover, using a template can help you identify a small piece of the project, giving you a starting point and helping develop momentum for the larger project. In fact, you should use templates even when you are not struggling with your writing. I find templates and examples useful in a wide variety of research projects to aid in wrapping my mind around a writing task.

JUST LIKE YOUR SCALE, YOUR CV DOESN'T TELL THE WHOLE STORY

Anyone who has ever been on a diet knows the frustration of spending weeks exercising and counting calories only to find that the scale refuses to budge. But your weight is just one indicator of your health, and while it is a metric you obviously want to keep an eye on, other metrics such as your body fat percentage or waist size can give you different insights into your health. The same holds true for your research and writing activities. If all you measure is the lines on your CV, you are missing some of the key metrics that help give you a strong CV in the first place. Focusing on your writing productivity, having clear goals for tenure, and establishing your research agenda are all key elements to having a tenure worthy vita. Clearly, having articles, books, and other publications are a necessary condition for getting tenure. You can spend time developing your agenda, setting aside writing time, and coming up with writing goals, but if you do not actually publish work, you will not get tenure. However, if you follow through on the ideas presented here, you will create the necessary conditions for a successful publishing career and build a strong foundation for your research efforts. The coin of the realm in most fields is published papers, but simply focusing on the need to publish a certain number of manuscripts does not give you concrete strategies. In the end, you want to see your hard work show up on the scale. Yet fixating on this point does not move you closer to this goal. My hope for you is to develop strategies and tactics to establish a strong publication record that will not only exceed the tenure expectations for your institution but will also set up a career of scholarly achievements.

REFERENCES

Altbach, P. G. (2013). Anarchy, commercialism, and "publish or perish". In P. G. Altbach (Ed.), *The International Imperative in Higher Education* (pp. 119–122). Rotterdam, NL: Sense Publishers.

Anderson, C., & Kilduff, G. (2009). Why do dominant personalities attain influence in face-to-face groups? The competence-signaling effects of trait dominance. *Journal of Personality and Social Psychology*, *96*(2), 491–503.

Bammer, G. (2008). Enhancing research collaborations: Three key managment challanges. *Research Policy*, *37*(5), 875–887.

Belcher, W. L. (2009). *Writing your journal article in twelve weeks: A guide to academic publishing success*. Thousand Oaks, CA: Sage.

Bentley, P., & Kyvik, S. (2011). Academic staff and public communication: A survey of popular science publishing across 13 countries. *Public Understanding of Science*, *20*(1), 48–63.

Boice, R. (1990). *Professors as writers: A self-help guide to productive writing*. Stillwater, OK: New Forums.

Boice, R. (1993). Writing blocks and tacit knowledge. *Journal of Higher Education*, *64*(1), 19–54.

Cain, S. (2013). *Quiet: The power of introverts in a world that can't stop talking*. New York, NY: Broadway Books.

Carson, R. D. (2003). *Taming your gremlin: A surprisingly simple method for getting out of your own way*. New York, NY: Harper Paperbacks.

Covey, S. R. (1990). *The seven habits of highly effective people*. New York, NY: Simon and Schuster.

Creamer, E. G. (2004). Collaborator's attitudes about difference of opinion. *Journal of Higher Education*, *75*(5), 556–571.

Creaser, C. (2010). Open access to research outputs-institutional policies and researchers' views: Results from two complementary surveys. *New Review of Academic Librarianships*, *16*(1), 4–25.

Cummings, J. N., & Hass, M. R. (2012). So many teams, so little time: Time allocation matters in geographically dispersed teams. *Journal of Organizational Behavior, 33*(3), 316–341.

Davidovitch, N. (2013). Learning-centered teaching and backward course design from transferring knowledge to teaching skills. *Journal of International Education Research, 9*(4), 329–338.

Dean, D. J., & Koster, J. B. (2014). *Equitable solutions for retaining a robust STEM workforce: Beyond best practices.* London: Academic Press.

Flaherty, A. W. (2005). *The midnight disease: The drive to write, writer's block, and the creative brain.* New York: Houghton Mifflin Harcourt.

Graf, C., Wager, E., Bowman, A., Fiack, S., Scott-Lichter, D., & Robinson, A. (2007). Best practice guidelines on publication ethics: A publisher's perspective. *International Journal of clinical practice, 61*(Suppl 152), 1–26.

Gravois, J. (2007). You're not fooling anyone. *The Chronicle of Higher Education.* Retrieved from http://www.chronicle.com/article/Youre-Not-Fooling-Anyone/28069

Gruzd, A., Staves, K., & Wilk, A. (2011). Tenure and promotion in the age of online social media. *Proceedings of the American Society for Information Science and Technology, 48*(1), 1–9.

Harley, D., & Acord, S. K. (2011). *Peer review in academic publishing: Its meaning, locus, and future.* Berkeley, CA: Center for Studies in Higher Education, University of California at Berkeley.

Hartley, J. (2008). *Academic writing and publishing: A practical handbook.* London, UK: Routledge.

He, Z.-L., Geng, X.-S., & Campbell-Hunt, C. (2009). Research collaboration and research output: A longitudinal study of 65 biomedical scientists in a New Zealand university. *Research Policy, 38*(2), 306–317.

Hossler, D., Lund, R. J., Westfall, S., & Irish, S. (1997). State funding for higher education: The sisyphean task. *Journal of Higher Education, 68*(2), 160–190.

Hundley, V., Van Teijlingen, E., & Simkhada, P. (2013). Academic authorship: Who, what and in what order? *Health Renaissance, 11*(2), 98–101.

Jance, J. A. (2016). It's Never Too Late. Retrieved from http://jajance.com/Blog/2016/11/11/its-never-too-late/

King, S. (2010). *On writing: A memoir of the craft.* New York: Pocket Books.

Lamott, A. (1994). *Bird by bird: Some instructions on writing and life.* New York: Anchor Books.

Larsen, P. O., & Von, M. (2010). The rate of growth in scientific publication and the decline in coverage by science citation index. *Scientometrics, 84*(3), 575–603.

Lee, S., & Bozeman, B. (2005). The impact of research collaboration on scientific productivity. *Social Studies of Science, 35*(5), 673–702.

Lovitts, B. E. (2005). Being a good course-taker not enough: A theoretical perspective on the transition to independent research. *Studies in Higher Education*, *30*(2), 137–154.

Lovitts, B. E. (2008). The transition to independent research: Who makes it who doesn't and why. *Journal of Higher Education*, *79*(3), 296–325.

Mehta, M. (2012). *The entrepreneurial instinct: How everyone has the innate ability to start a successful small business*. New York, NY: McGraw-Hill Education.

Moed, H. F. (2010). Measuring contextual citation impact of scientific journals. *Journal of informetrics*, *4*(3), 256–277.

Murray, R. (2013). *Writing for academic journals*. Maidenhead, UK: Open University Press.

National Institutes of Health. (2017). Research and training grants: Success rates by mechanism and selected activity codes. Retrieved from https://report.nih.gov/NIHDatabook/Charts/Default.aspx?showm=Y&chartId=275&catId=2

National Science Foundation. (2016). *Report to the National Science Board on the National Science Foundation's merit review process FiscalYear 2015*. Retrieved from Arlington, VA: www.nsf.gov/nsb/publications/2016/nsb201641.pdf

O'Meara, K. (2010). Rewarding multiple forms of scholarship: Promotion and tenure. In H. Fitzgerald, C. Burack, & S. Seifer (Eds.), *Handbook of engaged scholarship, volume 1: Institutional change* (pp. 271–294). East Lansing, MI: Michigan State University Press.

Reinsfelder, T. (2012). Open access publishing practices in a complex environment: Conditions, barriers, and bases of power. *Journal of Librarianship and Scholarly Communication*, *1*(1), 1–16.

Renfree, I., Harrison, D., Marshall, P., Stawarz, K., & Cox, A. (2016). *Don't kick the habit: The role of dependency in habit formation apps*. Paper presented at the CHI Conference Extended Abstracts on Human Factors in Computing Systems, Santa Clara, CA.

Rice, R. E., Sorcinelli, M. D., & Austin, A. E. (2000). *Heeding new voices: Academic careers for a new generation*. Washington, DC: American Association for Higher Education.

Richards, J. C. (2013). Curriculum approaches in language teaching: Forward, central, and backward design. *Relc Journal*, *44*(1), 5–33.

Schroter, S., & Tite, L. (2006). Open access publishing and author-pays business models: A survey of authors' knowledge and perceptions. *Journal of Royal Society Medicine*, *99*(3), 141–148.

Shaikh, A. (2015). A brief guide to research collaboration for the young scholar. Retrieved from www.elsevier.com/connect/a-brief-guide-to-research-collaboration-for-the-young-scholar

Silvia, P. J. (2007). *How to write a lot: A practical guide to productive academic writing*. Washington, DC: American Psychological Association.

Sonnenwald, D. H. (2007). Scientific collaboration. *Annual Review of Information Science and Technology*, *41*(1), 643–681.

Tandberg, D. A. (2010). Politics, interest groups and state funding of public higher education. *Research in Higher Education*, *51*(5), 416–450.

Uddin, S., Hossain, L., Abbasi, A., & Rasmussen, K. (2012). Trend and efficiency analysis of co-authorship network. *Scientometrics*, *90*(2), 987–699.

Zusman, A. (2005). Challanges facing higher education in the twenty-first century. In P. G. Altbach, R. O. Berdahl, & P. J. Gumport (Eds.), *American Higher Education in the Twenty-First Century: Social, political, and Economic Challenges* (pp. 115–160). Baltimore, MD: Johns Hopkins University Press.

Chapter 4

Teaching

Few assistant professors are truly prepared to enter the classroom. Graduate programs spend years preparing doctoral students for research, yet teaching often gets shortchanged. Maybe you served as a teaching or lab assistant or even had experience teaching your own classes, but I would consider yourself lucky if you received more than a short orientation to teaching. As a result, you may come into the teaching role with apprehension. Even if you were lucky enough to have taught several classes prior to becoming an assistant professor, each new institution and group of students can produce anxiety. Unfortunately, this apprehension and limited experience can prove particularly problematic during the pre-tenure years. Regardless of your level of teaching experience, I suspect you will face challenges balancing teaching with other demands, as well as challenges identifying strategies to improve your students' learning. Many assistant professors report spending an overwhelming amount of time preparing for classes and struggling to find their footing in the classroom (Hurtado, Eagan, Pryor, Whang, & Tran, 2012).

With little formal training in pedagogy, many faculty seek to model their teaching on faculty they enjoyed as students. The mantra is to replicate those teachers you enjoyed and do the opposite of the ones you did not. While there can be some value in copying approaches from outstanding faculty under whom you have studied, this should not be your sole approach to teaching. Research efforts by psychologists, neuroscientists, and educators have greatly increased our understanding of both how students learn and also best practices for teaching (Bain, 2011; Doyle & Zakrajsek, 2013; Nilson, 2010). In developing a teaching persona, I recommend not only including models from prior educational experiences, but also taking advantage of the rich literature on teaching and learning. It can prove helpful to establishing pedagogical approaches and course design processes, developing class policies, providing student feedback, and evaluating classes.

At the same time, teaching remains only one facet of an assistant professor's work, and all areas of faculty responsibility should be considered when planning teaching. If you are at an institution where teaching significantly impacts tenure, your time and commitment to it should look different than if teaching does not significantly impact your tenure review. However, this is not to suggest that, if you are a pre-tenure faculty member at a research university, you should completely neglect to improve your teaching. Great teaching may not get you tenure, but poor teaching certainly could keep you from it. Rather, I suggest thinking about teaching in the broader context of faculty work. You must adjust your management of teaching obligations, such as how you can build efficiency into your teaching activities, based on your institution's expectations. Certainly, I encourage all faculty to be strong and effective teachers. Yet, you must also consider the tenure expectations of your home department, university, and discipline when deciding how much time you can allocate to teaching.

As a new faculty member, you can immediately impact your department and students through teaching. Teaching offers the opportunity to leverage your expertise and share the knowledge you have gained during your many years of graduate study. As the saying goes, you do not really know something until you try to teach it. The challenge before you is to create a learning environment to *support* your students. This is the fundamental role of an instructor. You must identify learning outcomes, readings, lectures, class activities, and other elements to encourage and support your students' learning.

GETTING STARTED

If you are teaching for the first time or have limited experience, perhaps as a graduate teaching assistant, for example, the process of teaching can seem daunting, confusing, and full of unknowns. As with any new skill, you will get better the more that you teach, assuming you work at your craft. Even if you have significant teaching experience, however, learning about the expectations of your new institution, and the new student populations you may be working with, will raise new questions. Regardless of your teaching experience and comfort in the classroom, there are some specific strategies you can utilize to set yourself up for success.

No Need to Reinvent the Wheel

When assistant professors teach a class for the first time, they often fall into the trap of believing they need to start from scratch. Certainly, if you are hired to work in a new department or in a new area of study at your institution, you may be tasked with creating entirely new courses and material. In most cases, though, your teaching assignment will include courses that have been offered previously in your department or, at a minimum, in your graduate school department or at another institution. One of the first things you should do when starting work on a new course is to look at old syllabi. Seek out copies from previous iterations of the course you will be teaching. What textbooks were used? What assignments were given? You may not need to use these, but they will at least give you a starting place to understand how the course has been taught. In addition, talk to your colleagues about the class. Ideally, you could even discuss the course with a faculty member who taught it recently. These conversations can provide useful feedback and ideas for planning class, from the content to cover and the challenges you can anticipate to the experience and background in subject matter your students will have walking into your class. If you cannot find old syllabi from your department or a colleague who has worked with a class like this before, reach out to other departments and institutions similar to yours to seek their experiences and suggestions. Only in rare circumstances will a class be so new or different as to require you to completely reinvent the wheel. Take advantage of this fact to help ease the amount of work you'll need to do in preparation for class.

Everything But the Kitchen Sink

The biggest challenge pre-tenure faculty often face early in their teaching careers revolves around content. Many, and particularly new, faculty attempt to include far more content than is reasonable in a single course. As a result, the course can seem rushed, constantly behind, or provide limited student engagement because "there just isn't enough time." The reality, as the research literature clearly shows (Fulton, 2012; Roehl, Reddy, & Shannong, 2013), is that students are only able to absorb a limited amount of information in a single class session and over the course of a semester (Bunce, Flens, & Neiles, 2010). It may make you feel better as an instructor to rush through a lecture in order to cover all of your content, but students will not be able to successfully learn in this fashion. Instructors need to help students consolidate their learning and engage with course content in order to truly learn and meet their course objectives. Moreover, these objectives should drive content—not the other way around. As part of your teaching preparation prior to the semester or as part of earlier curriculum conversations with colleagues, you should establish clear course goals and learning objectives before you fine tune your content.

To be sure, learning objectives increasingly pervade the lexicon of higher education today, due in part to accreditation bodies and other outside groups (Beno, 2004; Ewell, 2001; Volkwein, Lattuca, Harper, & Domingo, 2007). In some cases, faculty have scoffed at the requirement to include them, as they feel these objectives serve more a regulatory compliance function rather than a teaching and learning one. Yet learning objectives can be incredibly helpful. Course learning objectives should drive the content you include. Setting aside their value in terms of accreditation or compliance, learning outcomes can help you focus on the content students need and narrow your course to allow you to explore key topics in more depth.

Let Course Policies Be Your Friend

If you have not already, you will quickly learn that students can be quite creative in their excuses and requests. Every semester, faculty witness everything from "the computer deleted my homework" to the epidemic of grandparents dying right before a major assignment is due. All kidding aside, a variety of legitimate concerns will arise during class, including some accompanied by documentation from various offices on campus—student health, disability services, etc. Particularly for inexperienced instructors, all of these requests, along with other decisions related to course procedures, can prove challenging. The best way to deal with these, and other issues, is to institute clear and consistent policies at the beginning of the semester. And at the end of the day, remember that it is okay to err on the side of students. Sure, someone may take advantage of your kindness, but it is important to remember your students are people with lives outside of your classes.

Course policies exist in two primary forms. First, your institution will require a series of policies to be included on all syllabi. Institutional policies often include areas such as academic dishonesty, nondiscrimination, drop/add dates, disability services, or final exam and reading day schedules. Instructors can check with the department chair, dean's office, or provost's office for the specific language required. You must seek out these policies to ensure you fulfill all the legal and compliance requirements at your institution.

Beyond the required institutional policies, you will determine the policies specific to your own classes. Course-specific policies should include requirements regarding attendance, participation, late work, and other specific expectations of student behavior. Instructors may include policies regarding the use of learning management systems (such as Blackboard or Canvas), evaluation and grading, homework policies, and other specifics regarding classwork. In addition, some instructors include policies regarding computers and mobile devices, although these are of debatable value (Lang, 2016a). Discussions with colleagues, reviewing previous syllabi, and thinking about potential class problems can all be fruitful strategies for outlining your policies. In the end, having a policy basis for decisions regarding your class will not only help provide a rationale for your decisions but will also offer your students transparency regarding your expectations.

Consult Your Campus Teaching Center

Most faculty do not hesitate to reach out to the grants or research office if they are considering applying for a grant. Everyone recognizes that the expertise

---

PAUSE AND REFLECT

Based on your prior teaching experience or discussions with friends and colleagues, what types of course policies should you include in your classes?

_____

_____

_____

_____

---

within these offices can be useful for putting together grant proposals and seeking funding. Unfortunately, faculty often do hesitate to reach out to their campus teaching centers, which similarly have expertise that can be useful for putting together courses. Teaching centers have a wealth of resources that can improve your teaching, save time, and help your students learn more. You will commonly find staff with experience and understanding of the research on college teaching. Centers provide workshops, training sessions, and one-on-one consultations to improve your teaching.

Despite the fact that these centers are staffed with people who get up every morning to help faculty, many are underutilized. Use this to your advantage! Ask for recommendations from your teaching center, have them observe one of your classes, and ask for their help using new technologies. These efforts need not be time intensive. For instance, a one hour consultation could provide you with a little nugget to improve your grading process that might save you hours of time over the next few years. Plus, your tenure committee will appreciate and recognize your professional development efforts when evaluating your teaching. Even if you doubt the potential benefits of meeting with your teaching center, your time and effort to do so will be recognized and will support the teaching element of your tenure case file. At a minimum, you will get credit for seeking professional development. More likely, you may discover a new technique that dramatically improves your instructional abilities and teaching efficiency.

First Things First

Finally, let's consider one of the biggest impacts on your experience teaching: the first day of class. You may be tempted to take attendance, give out your syllabus, and let your students go early. Instead, take James Lang's (2016b) advice to take advantage of the first day of class by using this unique opportunity to set the stage for the rest of the semester. Truly, you only get one chance to make a first impression. Below are some specific strategies to help make it a great one.

Arrive early: Give yourself time to set up the tables and chairs if they are moveable, get yourself prepared and comfortably situated, write any necessary messages on the board, or turn on and set up the projector and computer.

Learn students' names as quickly as possible: Start learning the names of your students (assuming the class is not very large). A photo roster, which many institutions allow faculty to download, can help with this both before and during class. Learning their names is a crucial first step in getting to know your students. The ability to call students by name communicates respects and helps them feel recognized as individuals. Additionally, using names may help draw out and involve quieter students in class discussions (Glentz, 2014).

Student introductions: Have students introduce themselves. Have them include something class related, such as: Why did you sign up for this class? What experience do you have relevant to the class content? What do you hope to learn? After you have a few students introduce themselves, pause and ask another member of the class to name all the students who have been introduced. You can then repeat this process until all students have been introduced and have had their names recalled. Conversely, you can have students write their names and a few facts about themselves, including any other pertinent information they need you to know, on a notecard (i.e., they are a student athlete, they have a learning disability, they have a subject sensitivity, etc.). This process creates a set of student flash cards you can use to learn names or reference later in the term. Of course, if your class is larger than 25–30 students, this may be hard to accomplish, but I still encourage you to get to know the students as much as possible.

Set the tone: This is crucial to the success of a class. You do not have to have a full class meeting, necessarily, but introduce students to the way class will be taught and to your style of teaching. If your class will include lectures with brief discussions, do at least a mini version of this on the first day.

Learn students' prior knowledge or experience: Create an activity to learn what prior knowledge or experience your students have related to your class. This information will prove useful for preparing future class sessions.

HOW TO PREP WELL

As you begin your teaching career, you will face some particular challenges as a new instructor. During the first two years of teaching, you must decide how to think about teaching preparation. In the early years of teaching everything will be new, from designing courses to creating class activities and preparing lecture notes. Making your class sessions effective and efficient can be especially challenging, particularly early in the pre-tenure years. While advice often suggests limiting teaching time, there are advantages to thinking about your teaching differently in your first few years compared to later in your career. One of the questions you should ask is whether it might be better to take additional time now to more thoroughly prepare courses than just attempting to get through the given class or semester.

When I talk about thorough preparation, I mean organizing, keeping good notes, and planning lessons in advance. For example, if you know you will teach an introductory course every semester for your first three years, a heavy initial investment in preparing for class could pay substantial dividends. Rather than creating a class activity just to have something to do that particular day, you can instead put in the planning ahead of time and then keep notes and other materials, making subsequent offerings of the same class easier to implement. For example, if I was teaching a heavily discussion based seminar, I would plan and store each day's discussion questions, along with notes about how the discussion went, for later reference. It makes more sense for me to take more time on the front end to think through the questions, write them down, and save them in a place that I can find them again, because then it will be easier to lead the discussion the next time around. Sometimes, taking this time will prove less helpful because you may not teach the class again or because the content changes substantially from semester to semester. However, the point is this: If you can more thoroughly make notes to yourself and prepare for classes in-depth the first time, you can save substantial preparation time in future semesters.

As any experienced teacher will tell you, the first or second time you teach a course is the most difficult. For this reason, you should attempt to limit your number of new class preparations prior to tenure. Obviously, new faculty will be required to teach some new classes, as this is part of the reason new faculty are hired. However, you should try to keep these as limited as possible. One rule of thumb is to look at what other new faculty in your department carry in terms of new preparations. In some cases, your department may require a limited number of preparations as the curriculum does not vary substantially from semester to semester or year to year. In other disciplines and departments, you may have a substantial number of new preparations due to the number of majors and graduate student level seminars offered. The bottom line is that you should limit the number of new class preparations to the extent practical. Fewer new class preparations will not only keep teaching time in line with other priorities, but will also allow time for you to improve courses that you have taught before.

Teaching a class multiple times allows you to take advantage of the work that you put in the first time preparing lectures, class activities and assessments. As the new faculty member in a department, you probably will not have a significant amount of influence over course schedules. However, the potential benefits to teaching the same class multiple times are worth requesting this opportunity from your department chair and senior faculty colleagues. Indeed, teaching a class multiple times can be one of the most effective teaching and time saving strategies I can recommend to you. Obviously, the amount of time you will need to prepare for class diminishes every time you teach it. While the time required does not drop to zero, of course, you can still realize some amazing efficiencies with the work you have done in prior semesters. Just like all other faculty responsibilities, you must consider class preparation within the proper context of all your priorities across teaching, research, and service. As indicated by your weekly time template from Chapter 2, you should have some idea of the amount of time available each week for teaching preparation, in line with your institution's expectations. Some faculty like to prep immediately prior to class, as this motivates them and provides a stopping point so that this time does not take over the entire week. Other faculty prefer to use their office hours, if sparsely attended, to prep. There is no right or wrong time to prep for teaching, so long as you effectively prepare for class and keep your efforts in line with your other faculty work.

For even more time savings, you can put in a significant amount of work prior to the semester with a little forethought and planning. If you are like me, you may need to prepare much of the reading for class closer to a particular class session, but you can plan activities and assignments further in advance. Especially if you have a higher teaching load, preparing significant chunks of your class prior to the semester can spread out your teaching obligations and carve out more time for research during the semester.

PAUSE AND REFLECT

Given the nature of the classes you teach, what could you prepare prior to the semester? Consider course design, assignments, assessments, and class activities.

_____

_____

_____

_____

_____

When thinking about preparing for class, I encourage you to purposefully consider how and when to complete this work. How can you increase efficiency by being organized? Can you take advantage of multiple offerings of the same course? Moreover, think about where teaching fits into your weekly schedule and have a plan for how to prepare for class. Finally, always remember to align your teaching prep with the tenure expectations at your institution.

THE POWER AND POTENTIAL OF ACTIVE LEARNING

In recent years, the use of active learning has grown dramatically, transforming college teaching (Fink, 2013). In simple terms, active learning comprises any instructional approach that moves beyond the student passively listening. Active learning teaching approaches have been mainstreamed thanks to significant empirical research showing their benefits (Barkley, Cross, & Major, 2014; Braxton, Jones, Hirschy, & Hartley, 2008; Bruff, 2009; Cavanagh, 2011; Eison, 2010; Freeman et al., 2014; Major, Harris, & Zakrajsek, 2015; Roehl et al., 2013; Ronchetti, 2010; Sarason & Banbury, 2004). However, many faculty have questions, concerns, or even a general distrust about utilizing active learning in their classrooms (Herrmann, 2013). Even students sometimes struggle with their role as an active participant in the learning process. In both my personal experience and as described in the teaching literature, many faculty still lecture as their primary teaching approach (Fry, Ketteridge, & Marshall, 2008; Svinicki & McKeachie, 2013). In the most emphatic terms possible, I encourage you to utilize active learning in each of your courses, from large introductory undergraduate courses to specialized graduate seminars. Research suggests that, to best engage students and promote learning, you must go beyond the traditional lecture (Ferreri & O'Connor, 2013). Active learning need not necessarily replace, in whole, the use of lectures, but it should at least augment this instructional approach (Harrington & Zakrajsek, 2017).

Active learning creates meaningful learning activities that push students to engage with course content and think critically about what they are learning (Bonwell & Eison, 1991; Braxton et al., 2008; Freeman et al., 2014; Gurung, 2002). When we contrast lectures with active learning, we can compare the degree to which students in each method are engaged in the learning process. In a traditional lecture, the learner passively listens and receives information from an instructor. In active learning, the learner adopts a more engaged posture to work *with* content, not just passively intake it (Bruff, 2009). In active learning, the instructor transitions from a deliverer of content to a designer of, and guide to, the learning environment. Active learning strategies range from simple, easy-to-implement in-class activities to complicated off-site experiences. Lord, Prince, Stefanou, and Stolk (2012) suggest that these strategies fall on a continuum ranging from instructor controlled, with interactive lectures, for example, to student controlled, with more open-ended design activities (role playing, in-class debates, etc.).

While your comfort level with active learning will dictate how much, and to what degree of complexity you decide to use such approaches in class, you should strive to incorporate at least one active learning strategy or activity per class session.

Before further discussing the benefits of active learning, I want to emphasize the advantages of lecturing. The lecture remains one of the most common teaching

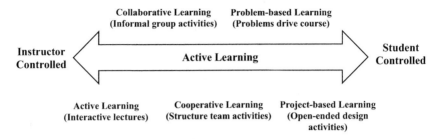

FIGURE 4.1 Active Learning Continuum

(Lord et al., 2012, p. 608)

approaches in large measure because it offers instructors maximum control over the information delivered in class (Van Klaveren, 2011). Moreover, lecturing showcases an instructor's expertise, which is rewarding, particularly for newly minted doctorates. From a learning perspective, lectures deliver the most immediate recall by students and offer the instructor the opportunity to bring content to life beyond what a student might read in the textbook. In his exhaustive meta-analysis, Bligh (1999) found that lectures proved as effective as other teaching methods for transmitting information.

Despite these benefits to lecture, research consistently shows that students who are more actively engaged demonstrate improved outcomes related to comprehending course content, problem solving, and critical thinking skills (Cavanagh, 2011). In most of the research comparing courses taught with lecture exclusively to courses taught with active learning techniques (Major et al., 2015), the evidence overwhelmingly supports active learning. Other recent studies suggest that incorporating active learning elements into lecture-based courses improves student learning (Eison, 2010). For instance, the use of "mini lectures" with active learning activities in between and guided note taking can meld the expanded learning opportunities of active learning within the comfort and tradition of lectures (Major et al., 2015).

Whether faculty embrace lecturing with an active engagement component or a fully active learning approach, I encourage all instructors to consider which activities can facilitate student engagement inside the classroom. The strongest activities are designed around important learning outcomes for your class and promote students' engagement with class material. As the research shows, well-designed activities support student learning and foster deeper levels of content knowledge (Freeman et al., 2014). Furthermore, a high level of student engagement both inside and outside the classroom predicts student success in college (Kuh, Cruce, Shoup, Kinzie, & Gonyea, 2008).

Active learning also provides other benefits. It is student focused; the deeper learning that occurs through active learning, after all, arises from student engagement rather than additional lecture time on a topic. Actively engaging with course material increases learning and betters conceptual understanding. In many cases, active learning class activities also benefit from the addition of collaborative learning. Decades of research show improved learning when students work with peers, (Cooper, Prescott, Cock, & Smith, 1990; Millis & Cottell, 1998; Millis, 2010). Students improve their academic achievement, retention, and social support by participating in collaborative learning opportunities (Barkley, 2009; Barkley et al., 2014; Major et al., 2015). Obviously, the ways students interact and collaborate differs based on class size, the nature of course content, and the classroom setup. However, broad support in the teaching and learning literature suggests finding ways for students to collaborate with wide-ranging student learning benefits (Bruffee, 1998; Rossing, Miller, Cecil, & Stamper, 2012). When designing class activities, there are three fundamental questions to ask:

1. *What am I trying to accomplish?* Identify the activity's objective, or what you want students to know at the end of class.
2. *How will I know that I have accomplished my goals?* For any activity, determine how students will demonstrate that they have met your goals.
3. *How will I know I am effective?* Class activities need components that allow you to assess student learning and provide feedback.

In *Teaching for Learning: 101 Intentionally Designed Educational Activities to Put Students on the Path to Success* (2015), my colleagues Claire Major, Todd Zakrajsek, and I identified a few considerations to incorporate when designing class activities. Use the worksheet below, adapted from our work, to practice utilizing these considerations in planning an in-class activity.

Each day brings more and more empirical research supporting effective teaching approaches, but the sheer number of journals and books makes it difficult for faculty to fully explore and utilize this literature. Luckily, your discipline likely has a journal dedicated to teaching in your field, such as the *Journal of Economic Education*, *Teaching Journalism & Mass Communication*, and *Journal of Teaching in Social Work*. Beyond journals and the works already mentioned, books such as Ken Bain's *What the Best College Teachers Do* (2011), *McKeachie's Teaching Tips* (Svinicki & McKeachie, 2013), James Lang's *Small Teaching* (2016b), and *Collaborative Learning Techniques* (Barkley et al., 2014) offer broad ranging advice. These resources can assist in constructing teaching and class activities that incorporate evidence-based teaching methods. As an added benefit, the research-based nature of this literature can support teaching effectiveness when building your case for tenure and promotion.

97

WORKSHEET 4.1 STEPS TO CREATING A SUCCESSFUL IN-CLASS ACTIVITY

Step 1. Overview of Activity

Write a brief description of your activity here. If you need help brainstorming ideas, consult *Teaching for Learning* or other teaching books mentioned in this chapter.

_____

_____

_____

_____

_____

Step 2. Determine Guiding Principles

Consider the learning principles that inform this activity. Thinking about guiding principles can inform how you plan to use the activity. For example, are you trying to access students' prior content knowledge or take advantage of experiential learning opportunities? Write your guiding principles here.

_____

_____

_____

_____

_____

Step 3. Preparation

Activities require varying levels of advance preparation. Make notes about what you need to do prior to class here.

_____

_____

_____

_____

_____

WORKSHEET 4.1 Continued

Step 4. Process

Write down the specific step-by-step instructions of the activity that you can use as lesson plans in class in the following space.

1) _____

2) _____

3) _____

4) _____

5) _____

Step 5. Tips for Next Time

Each time you use an activity, you learn something that can inform future uses. After class, write some brief notes to yourself to provide helpful tips for next time.

_____
_____
_____
_____
_____
_____
_____
_____
_____
_____
_____
_____
_____
_____
_____
_____

CREATING INCLUSIVE CLASSROOMS

In higher education classrooms across the country, student populations continue to change and become more culturally diverse. In this environment, it remains important for faculty, both seasoned and new, to consciously create inclusive classrooms (Schmeichel, 2012; Torres, Howard-Hamilton, & Cooper, 2003). This does not just happen on its own; without proactive efforts, certain student populations may feel alienated from the course or view its content as inaccessible (Gay, 2010; Wlodowski, 2011). An inclusive classroom is one in which a student feels his or her contributions and perspectives are respected and valued. This notion was more recently supported by Bryson and Hand (2007), who found that students were more likely to engage with course content if they felt supported by instructors who created inviting learning environments. Simple strategies can help create and maintain such an atmosphere.

In my classroom, I set ground rules from the start to ensure all students act with respect toward their peers. These ground rules help hold students accountable for their behavior. You can also set ground rules as an icebreaker activity during the first class meeting by having students create the rules together as a class (Brookfield & Preskill, 2005). Ask students to name the attributes of a productive learning environment, and develop a list of conditions required to achieve a successful and respectful semester.

You must also consider utilizing a variety of teaching strategies and activities to accommodate the needs of students with different backgrounds and abilities (Ambrose, Bridges, DiPietro, Lovett, & Norman, 2010). For instance, faculty can provide students with flexibility to demonstrate their knowledge by varying assessment strategies. On a final project, for example, you can allow students to pick their topic and explore an area of interest within the confines of the course content.

Cooperative learning techniques present another great way to create a flexible learning classroom. In cooperative learning, students are broken into small groups that encourage everyone to participate. If you are teaching a complex statistical concept to a group of first year students, for example, you may ask the students to solve a problem individually and then compare and discuss results in a small group. Or you might have students discuss the procedure for solving a problem in a small group and then solve the problem on their own. Working with peers encourages students to find different solutions and strategies for solving problems, and it helps them learn that there is not necessarily one right way to approach the content. Also, students may feel more motivated and successful within small groups because the group dynamic increases their perception of their ability to complete the task working together (Johnson & Johnson, 1999). These activities consciously incorporate a variety of learning preferences and options for participation, which in turn helps to create an environment that feels accessible to all students.

GRADING STUDENT WORK: A NECESSARY EVIL

I think few faculty truly enjoy the process of grading student work; nevertheless, grading and student feedback remain a substantial component of the teaching process. During the first few years of teaching, developing assignments, grading processes, and establishing expectations for student work will be a time-intensive and challenging aspect of an assistant professor's job. Some specific strategies and techniques can improve grading efficiency and provide useful feedback to students, yet there is no way around the reality that grading will require a significant amount of teaching time.

The grading process begins long before you actually sit down to grade students' work. As part of the very initial course design, in fact, you must think through the types of evaluation and assignments needed for class. Will you use tests or quizzes to gauge student comprehension? Will you require students to write essays and research papers? Will you grade student participation? If so, how? Will the course focus on just one type of evaluation (such as exams) or multiple? Make sure that you will be able to appropriately assess how students learn in your course. In addition to changing the assessment's quantitative value, you will need to vary the amount of feedback for different types of assignments. Some assignments only require a completion check or pass/fail grade, while others require extensive feedback and comments. Moreover, consider the timing of assignments in light of other expectations. For example, you can vary the due dates or the types of assignments across your courses to minimize grading crunches. If you have research papers due in one class, for example, then you can assign your other class a pass/fail assignment due the same week. At the start of each semester, look at a list of all your draft class assignments to see how you can balance your grading. To be sure, if you are in a discipline with heavy writing requirements such as English or other humanities disciplines, there is only so much you can do on this point. However, in many cases, pre-planning can save you a great deal of stress later in the semester.

Providing Student Feedback

Beyond the types of assignments and due dates, establishing grading criteria is a critical part of planning for the semester. What type of grading scale will you use? Will you give out letter grades, number grades, or points? Faculty often make their grading far more difficult by over-engineering their classes, particularly in weighting grades. Of course, you will likely want to weight assignments differently based on their significance to your course, the amount of effort required for students, and other factors. Yet, be careful to not over complicate your system. I once worked with a faculty member who had a 290-point scale for class. As part of the class, quizzes were graded on a 1–10 scale. She assigned 5 quizzes during the semester, with a total point value of 75. Her students were confused and, frankly, so was she. Weighting grades is necessary and valuable, but err on the side of simple to help both you and your students. Also, let technology assist you with calculating grades by using a spreadsheet or your campus' learning management system to avoid simple arithmetic errors.

In addition to pre-determining your grading scales, identifying the most important criteria for student work prior to the semester will provide a degree of clarity for students, promote a sense of fairness, and save you time in the grading process. For each assignment, what is most important to you in evaluating student work? Do you want to see creativity, mastery of course content, and/or appropriate writing such as clarity or grammar? Grading plays a few different roles in terms of instruction, including serving as an indicator of performance in class and providing feedback to students (Walvoord & Anderson, 2010). Depending on your class and the assignment, rubrics can share clear guidelines and expectations with students and limit your time grading (Andrade, 2005; Malini & Andrade, 2010). While rubrics hold some potential, I caution against using them ineffectively which can make assignments overly formulaic or restrict your ability to offer students a holistic review of their work (Malini & Andrade, 2010; Panadero & Jonsson, 2013). Regardless of whether you use rubrics, you must establish criteria for how students will complete their work on specific assignments. Do you want students to use a particular font or other formatting elements? Do you want hard copy submissions or electronic ones? For instance, I set strict and consistent requirements on file names and types for electronically submitted work. Students are required to send me a Microsoft Word file named with their last name and the name of the assignment. This format helps me keep track of submitted assignments; otherwise, everyone would turn in a file named "Essay 1" and I would have no idea how to tell them apart without opening each file.

When it is time to sit down and grade your students' assignments, plan ahead but be willing to experiment with your grading process. Are you going to grade the assignments alphabetically, in the order that they were turned in, or from the best to worst students? Are you going to grade students blind or do you want to know whose assignment you are grading? Can you complete grading in a single session or do you need to spread it out over several days? Establish a goal for how long you want to spend on each assignment to set a pace for yourself. Once you establish this goal, time yourself and work really hard to stick to the time allotted. Especially if you are new to grading, you will be tempted to spend 2–3 times longer than you hope on grading. However, there are some ways that you can seek to limit your grading time while still providing useful feedback to your students.

Your feedback should focus on things your students can learn and improve in the future. We all have a natural tendency to want to provide comments to justify our grades. While this is understandable, the reality is that, if your assignments are focused on learning goals and your comments are focused on how to help students learn for the future, you will be providing sufficient justification. Students may still complain or question your evaluation, but you will have plenty evidence to stand on by focusing your feedback on improvement and learning. Be careful to avoid *over* commenting on student work. You may feel that identifying every mistake can only help, but it will likely just overwhelm. Especially with grammar and punctuation issues, you may be tempted to begin line-editing your students' papers. Don't. As Brookhart (2011) suggests, less is often more in student feedback. Instead of noting every single problem, look for major trends and patterns to address. Then, you can note the pattern once with explanation and quickly note other instances without having to explain each in detail. The goal is to only make a detailed comment once, then simply highlight additional occurrences. Finally, when providing summative feedback to students, make use of the sandwich method of providing constructive criticism.

Despite your best efforts, you will be unable to avoid student criticism and complaints regarding your grading. Students view grades differently than in the past, thanks to the regime of high-stakes testing dominating education today, particularly in K-12 (Au, 2007; Heilig & Darling-Hammond, 2008; Jacobs, 2005). Experience with high-stakes testing leads students to seek high grades, get the "right" answer, and question constructive criticism (Horn, 2003; Hursh, 2008). However, you can try a few strategies to mitigate student complaints regarding grades. First and foremost, be as transparent as possible. By clearly identifying and communicating your expectations and policies early on, you will be able to limit many concerns. Additionally, set aside some in-class time to discuss upcoming major assignments and assessments, rather than simply posting instructions online, including them in the syllabus on the first day of class, or providing a handout as students leave the room. And repeat this time if necessary as students work their way through major projects. The first or last 5–10 minutes of class can prove a good space to gauge student progress on important assignments.

Although this may seem antithetical to transparency, you should avoid discussing grades in class. While I may provide some overall feedback on how the class performed on a particular assignment, I do not make comments such as, "Only

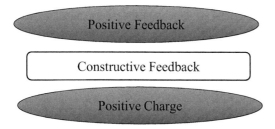

FIGURE 4.2 Sandwich Method (constructive feedback)

two people got A's on this paper," or, "I was disappointed in the grades on the midterm exam." I find that the more I talk about grades, particularly in a negative way, the more likely I am to get students thinking about grades in a negative light. Additionally, avoid discussing grades and student complaints for 24 hours after distributing graded work. This "cooling off" period allows students to articulate any questions they may have without the immediate emotion of discovering a disappointing grade. I have found that many students, upon reflection, realize that they do not even need to discuss their work. At the end of the day, students will complain about grades and have questions about your feedback. Stick to the policies you have made clear from the beginning of class, seek guidance from your colleagues and department chair, and do not take questioning personally. Grading and providing student feedback may not be the most fun part of the job, but is a critical part of your role as an instructor.

COURSE EVALUATIONS

There is one area of teaching related to tenure that creates more controversy than nearly any other: student course evaluations. Many times, course evaluations constitute one of, if not the only quantitative metric, that we have to evaluate the teaching quality of pre-tenure faculty. Often, professors decry course evaluations as hopelessly biased, based on superficial factors, and lacking in reliability. Despite these concerns, student evaluations remain key in tenure committees' determinations of teaching quality. Research on course evaluations provides some insight into their strengths and weaknesses. For example, Barre (2015) found that evaluations offer a valid measure of learning and help students examine the learning environment of class. Over 25 years of research on student evaluations shows that they are best able to provide the student's view on his or her learning experience (Cohen, 1981). The literature responds less clearly to many of the complaints raised by critics. Stark and Freishtat (2014) raised issues of methodological concern, while other authors have found evaluations can be influenced by course grades (Worthington, 2002), gender (Anderson & Miller, 1997), and instructor attractiveness (Ambady & Rosenthal, 1993) among other concerns.

While the merits of course evaluations are much debated in higher education teaching and learning, there is little debate that they are overwhelmingly used by tenure committees when evaluating an assistant professor's work in the classroom (Galbraith, Merrill, & Kline, 2012; Nasser & Fresko, 2002). In research universities, senior colleagues frequently advise that student teaching evaluations should be above the department average. Perhaps attempting to prove the Lake Wobegon notion that "everyone can be above average," tenure committees commonly look for above-average scores and student comments indicating that an instructor is engaged, taking their teaching seriously, and are available and approachable for students. In institutions where teaching more greatly impacts the tenure decision, course evaluations are considered in even more depth and with more nuance than at a research university. For example, you can expect tenure committees to look at your evaluation scores for one class relative to other classes you have taught, consider the types of students you are working with, and examine in much greater detail the written feedback from your students. Tenure committees will try to triangulate this information with other teaching related materials included in your dossier such as your teaching philosophy, teaching observation reports, and other student feedback.

Given all the research and debate surrounding course evaluations, I suggest you place them in the proper context. Course evaluations will matter in your tenure review, but it is unlikely that they will decide your fate. Even if your student evaluations are quite low, tenure committees will likely look for other evidence to confirm or justify a low estimation of your teaching abilities before denying tenure. While it is natural to eagerly await your student evaluations— and I encourage you to take them seriously—I caution against obsessing about high or low results. Evaluations are *one* piece of evidence for you and your tenure committee, but they should and most likely will never be the *only* source of information regarding your teaching.

Depending on your discipline and graduate institution, you may already have experience with course evaluations as a teaching assistant or lecturer. Or this may be the first time you receive this type of feedback. Even after all the years that I have been teaching, I still eagerly open my course evaluations to see feedback from my students. There are so few times in faculty work when we receive direct feedback, and course evaluations, to me, have always seemed like a welcome source of information. However, I strongly suggest you approach course evaluations in a logical manner to frame what you are hearing—and not hearing— from your students. Specifically, I recommend four points when reviewing your course valuations: 1) look for patterns, 2) cut yourself some slack, 3) seek a second opinion, and 4) supplement evaluations.

1. Look for Patterns

Patterns are the most useful data you can find in your course evaluations. As you review your results, look across all your courses and especially multiple offerings of the same course. Many times in my career I have had a few students, or the entire class, provide responses that seemed off the wall or incorrect to me. While you never want to completely dismiss feedback from an entire class, we all know that sometimes classes just do not work well for a variety of reasons. However, if you start to see patterns in your evaluations, then you can start to reasonably assume an issue is real and warrants attention in future iterations of the class. For example, early in my career, I was teaching a course with two textbooks. I liked the differing views that each textbook brought to the table, but I struggled with exactly matching up the readings each week. While I thought I had found the sweet spot incorporating the readings, I received feedback on my evaluations proving that students still felt the disconnect. I decided to try again the following semester, but after I got almost identical feedback, I came to realize the two books were not working as well as I hoped. As a result, I decided to include a couple of chapters from the second text rather than requiring the entire book.

2. Cut Yourself Some Slack

Every semester you will likely get a few comments from students who think you are the absolute worst professor that they have ever had, and you will probably also get some feedback from some students who think you walk on water. Remember this: You are never as good or bad as your most extreme student responses. Follow the old political advice to never read your own press clippings. I always frame outlier responses like in Olympics sports, where the highest and lowest scores are thrown out to calculate the final results. You will need to do the same thing with your student evaluations. Ignore the most glowing and the most damning responses. Instead, focus on the middle responses that likely provide the best measure for how most students responded to your class and instruction.

3. Seek a Second Opinion

Depending on the culture of your department, course evaluations may be discussed a great deal or not at all. At times, you can benefit substantially from getting a second opinion. Many faculty, both on the tenure track and not, take their course evaluation feedback quite personally. I think this can be of value, since it shows how much you care about your teaching. However, these feelings present a challenge for you to step back and carefully consider the feedback that you received from your students. I frequently have conversations with faculty who are worked up about some feedback in their course evaluations, but when I asked how they thought class went they provide almost the same feedback. Sometimes, you just need someone to help you see the bigger picture. Seeking out a trusted colleague for second opinion can be enormously helpful when reviewing your course evaluation results.

4. Supplemental Evaluations Can Provide Balance

With the pros and cons of student evaluations, research suggests supplementing them with other feedback to create a more rounded picture of your course (Spooren, Brockx, & Mortelmans, 2013). Personally, I often use supplemental course evaluations conducted in the middle of the term or at the end of the semester. Midcourse evaluations provide baseline data that I can compare to my end of course evaluations. You might include only one or two questions, such as what a student likes most about your course and what they wish was different. Or you could make your midcourse evaluation quite complex, including detailed questions about the course content and your instruction or asking in advance questions that students will see at the end of the semester (Creamer, 2004).

The greatest benefit of supplemental evaluations, no matter when you offer them, is that they can provide answers to questions not included on university-sponsored course evaluations. For instance, I might ask students about specific readings or class activities. I may ask about their learning of a particular content area that might help me judge how they comprehended class content. Course evaluations provided by the university can rarely get at these specifics. In addition, supplemental evaluations provide another data point to include in your tenure materials. The data from them can be used to provide further evidence in support of the data already gathered by your university course evaluations, or to help contextualize lower scores. A second supplemental option is to invite a colleague into your class to observe your teaching and offer formative and/or summative feedback, which can provide useful evidence to support your teaching case. In the end, course evaluations play an important role in how your teaching is evaluated for tenure, but they more significantly can provide useful data to improve the quality of your teaching.

CONCLUSION

Too often, I fear pre-tenure faculty receive the advice that teaching does not matter in the tenure process. While this is certainly not true at teaching-oriented universities, this advice is problematic even in situations where research forms the primary basis for a tenure decision. Instead, all faculty across the various types of colleges and universities should undertake teaching with the seriousness it deserves. I never suggest that faculty shirk their teaching responsibilities to steal away time for more research or other activities. While we all know faculty who treat teaching as a mere obligation, conceptualizing it in this way disserves our students.

However, I do agree with those who argue that teaching can take up too much time relative to other faculty responsibilities. My argument to pre-tenure faculty is to seek efficiencies in teaching that also maximize student learning. The advice in this chapter, to realize the benefits of active learning and proactively plan teaching preparation time, is consistent with this goal. No matter the weight of teaching in the tenure process at your particular institution, you should leverage the research on college teaching to realize efficiency and student-centered learning. Finally, understand that teaching is a craft that you will better over time. In fact, tenure committees will reward you for refining your teaching, seeking professional development opportunities, and improving your instructional practices. Just as students enter class as novices, many pre-tenure faculty come into the classroom as novice teachers. With thoughtful reflection, practice, and guidance from peers and mentors, however, you can improve your teaching and provide the evidence of high quality instruction necessary to receive tenure.

REFERENCES

Ambady, N., & Rosenthal, R. (1993). Half a minute: Predicting teacher evaluations from thin slices of nonverbal behavior and physical attractiveness. *Journal of Personality and Social Psychology*, *64*(3), 431.

Ambrose, S. A., Bridges, M. W., DiPietro, M., Lovett, M. C., & Norman, M. K. (2010). *How learning works: Seven research-based principles for smart teaching.* San Francisco, CA: Jossey-Bass.

Anderson, K., & Miller, E. D. (1997). Gender and student evaluations of teaching. *PS: Political Science and Politics*, *30*(2), 216–219.

Andrade, H. G. (2005). Teaching with rubrics: The good, the bad, and the ugly. *College Teaching*, *53*(1), 27–31.

Au, W. (2007). High-stakes testing and curricular control: A qualitative metasynthesis. *Educational Researcher*, *36*(5), 258–267.

Bain, K. (2011). *What the best college teachers do.* Cambridge, MA: Harvard University Press.

Barkley, E. F. (2009). *Student engagement techniques: A handbook for college faculty.* San Francisco, CA: Jossey-Bass.

Barkley, E. F., Cross, K. P., & Major, C. H. (2014). *Collaborative learning techniques: A handbook for college faculty* (1st ed.). San Francisco, CA: Jossey-Bass.

Barre, E. (2015). Do student evaluations of teaching really get an "F"? Retrieved from http://cte.rice.edu/blogarchive/2015/07/09/studentevaluations

Beno, B. A. (2004). The role of student learning outcomes in accreditation quality review. *New Directions for Community Colleges*, *126*, 65–72.

Bligh, D. A. (1999). *What's the use of lectures?* San Francisco, CA: Jossey-Bass.

Bonwell, C. C., & Eison, J. A. (1991). *Active learning: Creating excitement in the classroom.* Washington, DC: The George Washington University.

Braxton, J. M., Jones, W. A., Hirschy, A. S., & Hartley, H. V. (2008). The role of active learning in college persistence. *New Directions for Teaching and Learning*, *115*, 71–83.

Brookfield, S. D., & Preskill, S. (2005). *Discussion as a way of teaching: Tools and techniques for democratic classrooms.* San Francisco, CA: Jossey-Bass.

Brookhart, S. M. (2011). Tailoring feedback. *The Educational Digest*, *76*(9), 33–36.

Bruff, D. (2009). *Teaching with classroom response systems: Creating active learning environments.* San Francisco, CA: Jossey-Bass.

Bruffee, K. A. (1998). *Collaborative learning: Higher education, interdependence, and the authority of knowledge.* Baltimore, MD: Johns Hopkins University Press.

Bryson, C., & Hand, L. (2007). The role of engagement in inspiring teaching and learning. *Innovations in Education and Teaching International, 44*(4), 349–362.

Bunce, D. M., Flens, E. A., & Neiles, K. Y. (2010). How long can students pay attention in class? A study of student attention decline using clickers. *Journal of Chemical Education, 87*(12), 1438–1443.

Cavanagh, M. (2011). Students' experiences of active engagment through cooperative learning activities in lectures. *Active Learning in Higher Education, 12*(1), 23–33.

Cohen, P. A. (1981). Student ratings of instruction and student achievement: A meta-analysis of multisection validity studies. *Review of Educational Research, 51*(3), 281–309.

Cooper, J., Prescott, S., Cock, L., & Smith, L. (1990). *Cooperative learning and college instruction: Effective use of learning teams.* Dominguez Hills, CA: The California State University.

Creamer, E. G. (2004). Collaborator's attitudes about difference of opinion. *Journal of Higher Education, 75*(5), 556–571.

Doyle, T., & Zakrajsek, T. (2013). *The new science of learning: How to learn in harmony with your brain.* Sterling, VA: Stylus Publishing.

Eison, J. (2010). Using active learning instructional strategies to create excitement and enchance learning. *Jurnal Pendidikantentang Strategi Pembleajaran Aktif (Active Learning) Books, 2*(1), 1–10.

Ewell, P. T. (2001). *Accreditation and student learning outcomes: A proposed point of departure.* Washington, D.C.: Council for Higher Education Accreditation.

Ferreri, S., & O'Connor, S. K. (2013). Instructional design and assessment: Redesign of a large lecture course into a small-group learning course. *American Journal of Pharmaceutical Education, 77*(1), 1–9.

Fink, D. (2013). *Creating significant learning experiences: An integrated approach to designing courses.* San Francisco, CA: Jossey-Bass.

Freeman, S., Eddy, S. L., McDonough, M., Smith, M. K., Okoroafor, N., Jordt, H., & Wenderoth, M. P. (2014). Active learning increases student performance in science, engineering, and mathematics. *Proceedings of the National Academy of Sciences of the United States of America, 111*(23), 8410–8415.

Fry, H., Ketteridge, S., & Marshall, S. (2008). *A handbook for teaching and learning in higher education: Enhancing academic practice* (3rd ed.). New York, NY: Routledge.

Fulton, K. (2012). Upside down and inside out: Flip classroom to improve student learning. *Learning and Leading with Technology, 39*(8), 12–17.

Galbraith, C., Merrill, G., & Kline, D. (2012). Are student evaluations of teaching effectiveness valid for measuring student outcomes in business related classes? A neural network and Bayesian analyses. *Research in Higher Education, 53*, 353–374.

Gay, G. (2010). *Culturally responsive teaching: Theory, research, and practice*. New York, NY: Teachers College Press.

Glentz, T. (2014). The importance of learning students' names. *Journal on Best Teaching Practices, 1*(1), 21–22.

Gurung, R. (2002). Sleeping students don't talk (or Learning: Enhancing active learning via class participation. In P. Price (Ed.), *Active learning in the classroom: Overview and methods*. New Orleans, LA: Symposium conducted at the 14th annual meeting of the American Psychology Society.

Harrington, C., & Zakrajsek, T. (2017). *Dynamic lecturing: Research-based strategies to enhance lecture effectiveness*. Sterling, VA: Stylus Publishing.

Heilig, J. V., & Darling-Hammond, L. (2008). Accountability Texas-style: The progress and learning of urban minortity students in a high-stakes testing context. *Educational Evaluation and Policy Analysis, 30*(2), 75–110.

Herrmann, K. J. (2013). The impact of cooperative learning on student engagement: Results from an intervention. *Active Learning in Higher Education, 14*(3), 175–187.

Horn, C. (2003). High-stakes testing and students: Stopping or perpetuating a cycle of failure. *Theory into Practice, 41*(1), 30–41.

Hursh, D. W. (2008). *High-stakes testing and the decline of teaching and learning: The real crisis in education* (Vol. 1). Lanham, MD: Rowman & Littlefield.

Hurtado, S., Eagan, K., Pryor, J. H., Whang, H., & Tran, S. (2012). Undergraduate teaching faculty: The 2010–2011 HERI faculty survey. University of California, Los Angeles, CA: Higher Education Research Institute.

Jacobs, B. A. (2005). Accountability, incentives and behavior: The impact of high-stakes testing in Chicago public schools. *Journal of Public Economics, 89*(5), 761–796.

Johnson, D. W., & Johnson, R. T. (1999). *Learning together and alone: Cooperative, competitive, and individualistic learning*. Boston, MA: Allyn and Bacon.

Kuh, G. D., Cruce, T. M., Shoup, R., Kinzie, J., & Gonyea, R. M. (2008). Unmasking the effects of student engagement on first-year college grades and persistence. *Journal of Higher Education, 79*(5), 540–563.

Lang, J. M. (2016a, September 11). No, banning laptops is not the answer. *The Chronicle of Higher Education*. Retrieved from www.chronicle.com/article/No-Banning-Laptops-Is-Not-the/237752

Lang, J. M. (2016b). *Small teaching: Everyday lessons from the science of learning*. San Francisco, CA: Jossey-Bass.

Lord, S. M., Prince, M. J., Stefanou, C. R., & Stolk, J. D. (2012). The effect of different active learning environments on student outcomes related to lifelong learning. *International Journal of Engineering Education, 26*(3), 608.

Major, C. H., Harris, M. S., & Zakrajsek, T. (2015). *Teaching for learning: 101 intentionally designed educational activities to put students on the path to success*. New York, NY: Routledge.

Malini, R., & Andrade, H. (2010). A review of rubric use in higher education. *Assessment & Evaluation in Higher Education, 35*(4), 435–448.

Millis, B., & Cottell, P. (1998). *Cooperative learning for higher education faculty.* Cincinnati, OH: Oryx Press.

Millis, B. J. (Ed.). (2010). *Cooperative learning in higher education: Across the disciplines, across the academy.* Sterling, VA: Stylus.

Nasser, F., & Fresko, B. (2002). Faculty views of student evaluation of college teaching. *Assessment & Evaluation in Higher Education, 27*(2), 187–198.

Nilson, L. B. (2010). *Teaching at its best: A research-based resource for college instructors.* San Francisco, CA: Jossey-Bass.

Panadero, E., & Jonsson, A. (2013). The use of scoring rubrics for formative assessment purposes revisted: A review. *Educational Research Review, 9,* 129–144.

Roehl, A., Reddy, S. L., & Shannong, G. J. (2013). The flipped classroom: An opportunity to engage millennial students through active learning. *Journal of Family Consumer Sciences, 105*(2), 44–49.

Ronchetti, M. (2010). Using video lectures to make teaching more interactive. *International Journal of Emerging Technologies in Learning, 5*(2), 45–48.

Rossing, J. P., Miller, W. M., Cecil, A. K., & Stamper, S. E. (2012). iLearning: The future of higher education? Student perceptions on learning with mobile tablets. *Journal of the Scholarship of Teaching and Learning, 12*(2), 1–26.

Sarason, Y., & Banbury, C. (2004). Active learning facilitated by using a game show format or who doesn't want to be a millionaire? *Journal of Management Education, 28*(4), 509–518.

Schmeichel, M. (2012). Good Teaching? An examination of culturally relevant pedagogy as an equity practice. *Journal of Curriculum Studies, 44*(2), 211–231.

Spooren, P., Brockx, B., & Mortelmans, D. (2013). On the validity of student evaluation of teaching: The state of the art. *Review of Educational Research, 83*(4), 598–642.

Stark, P. B., & Freishtat, R. (2014). *An evaluation of course evaluations.* Retrieved from www.stat.berkeley.edu/~stark/Preprints/evaluations14.pdf

Svinicki, M., & McKeachie, W. J. (2013). *McKeachie's teaching tips: Strategies, research, and theory for college and university teachers* (14th ed.). Belmont, CA: Cengage Learning.

Torres, V., Howard-Hamilton, M. F., & Cooper, D. L. (2003). *Identity development of diverse populations: Implications for teaching and administration in higher education* (Vol. 29). San Francisco, CA: Jossey-Bass.

Van Klaveren, C. (2011). Lecturing style teaching and student performance. *Economics of Education Review, 30*(4), 729–739.

Volkwein, J. F., Lattuca, L. R., Harper, B. J., & Domingo, R. J. (2007). Measuring the impact of professional accreditation on student experiences and learning outcomes. *Research in Higher Education, 48*(2), 251–282.

Walvoord, B. E., & Anderson, V. J. (2010). *Effective grading: A tool for learning and assessment in college*. San Francisco, CA: Jossey-Bass.

Wlodowski, R. J. (2011). *Enhancing adult motivation to learn: A comprehensive guide for teaching all adults*. New York, NY: John Wiley & Sons.

Worthington, A. C. (2002). The impact of student perceptions and characteristics on teaching evaluations: A case study in finance education. *Assessment and Evaluation in Higher Education, 27*(1), 49–64.

Chapter 5

Service

Higher education depends on faculty serving as academic citizens (McMillin & Berberet, 2002; Ward, 2003). The entire enterprise requires faculty to serve in order to function (Brew, Boud, Lucas, & Crawford, 2017; Lawrence, Ott, & Bell, 2012). Without service, there would be no peer review, professional associations, or committees completing important work like faculty hiring, student admissions, and curricular oversight (Ward, 2003). As famed medical doctor and scientist Jonas Salk once said, "The reward for work well done is the opportunity to do more." While higher education needs faculty as academic citizens, service can be fraught for pre-tenure faculty (Ponjuan, Conley, & Trower, 2011). Service constitutes just a minor aspect of the tenure case, despite the amount of time it can take up (Holland, 2016). Moreover, service is difficult to define and quantify, which can complicate your ability to demonstrate its extent and impact during the tenure process (Bensimon, Ward, & Sanders, 2000; Neumann & Terosky, 2007).

In the context of tenure, service includes professional activities that support the governance and management of the department, school, institution, and discipline. Moreover, service refers to activities completed outside of your regular teaching and research responsibilities to support the operations of your institution or discipline (Finsen, 2002). You may hear advice from senior colleagues and mentors that you need to say "no" to service. This suggestion stems from the fact that service plays only a small role in how committees evaluate tenure cases— and this belief is often reflected in how the institutions deprioritize service involvement (Hardre, Beesley, Miller, & Pace, 2011). Tenure review committees *do* want to see pre-tenure faculty play a part in the life of the institution and discipline; a complete failure to do so will raise a red flag. However, most mentors, myself included, think assistant professors spend too much time on their service to the detriment of scholarship and teaching activities.

Pre-tenure faculty need to complete just enough service to be a team player, but not so much that it eclipses the primary areas of faculty work valued in the tenure process. Moreover, what constitutes "being a team player" can vary based on the research and publishing expectations at your institution. As a general rule, higher research expectations lead to lower service expectations. For example, institutions emphasizing teaching will likely ask you to take on service responsibilities related to teaching such as advising students or assessment and curriculum review. In these institutions, failing to fulfill your service may also be seen as failing to fulfill your teaching responsibilities, which can be quite harmful to your tenure case. A major exception to this rule, however, exists at many "striving" institutions. These traditionally teaching focused institutions, in attempting to grow their research profile, often strap assistant professors with significant service and teaching loads while at the same time increasing requirements for scholarship (O'Meara, 2007, 2010).

Another significant variation in service during the pre-tenure years is the degree to which your academic department generally, and your department chair specifically, protects tenure candidates from excessive service requests. This will depend more on departmental culture than on institutional or discipline differences (Tierney & Rhoads, 1994). For instance, a chemistry department in one institution may be quite protective of pre-tenure faculty, while another chemistry department may not have a similar culture of support. Often, departments within the same school have dramatically different cultures and values around service expectations (Misra, Lundquist, Holmes, & Agiomavritis, 2011). In fact, you should attempt to determine these expectations during your job search process. Often, departments with a positive culture regarding service will bring it up during the search in order to recruit you. If, however, you do not hear anything about pre-tenure service, you should definitely find out as much as possible. Ask what the department chair and tenure committees expect in terms of service for tenure. If you get a generic response, ask about the service commitments of a recently tenured faculty member in the department or school. Obviously, the worst-case scenario is a department that not only fails to protect you from service but actively requires too much service.

During my pre-tenure years, I took on an incredible amount of service as the result of two factors working against me. First, there were the attributes of my program: It was relatively small, had a large number of students, and was introducing a new degree program. As a result, there were plentiful meetings, many students to advise, and lots of administrative work to be completed. Second, I genuinely enjoyed administrative work and found it more rewarding than some of my teaching or research activities, especially during the first two years while I was establishing myself as a researcher and teacher. While I knew intellectually that service was not going to get me tenure, I still spent too much time and effort on these activities. Fortunately, thanks to advice from mentors and colleagues as well as a stern conversation with myself, I redoubled my efforts with scholarship.

This put me back on the right track. Specifically, I scaled back my committee work, stepping back from a few big groups as well as declining other offers that came in before tenure. Additionally, I began to protect my time and schedule advising meetings and other activities no more than four hours per week. Once those hours were booked, I pushed meetings back rather than giving up research time. After I received tenure, I learned from a colleague that one of my external reviewers took my institution to task for giving me too much service during my first few years on the tenure track. While I agree that my institution expected too much service from its assistant professors, I too was responsible for not spending the appropriate time on activities central to my tenure case. This experience is one of the reasons I strongly advocate managing your time across all areas of faculty work and developing a weekly template (see Chapter 2).

The lesson here is that, whether you enjoy service or not, it can derail your tenure and promotion case. While you will want to engage in personally and professionally rewarding activities, which can certainly include service, I caution you to consider service through the lens of your tenure review committees. To this day, I enjoy service and administrative work much more than many of my colleagues; I have even taken a part-time administrative role directing my university's teaching center. At this point, I can afford to pursue administrative work because I do not have the same expectations placed on me as I did when I was working toward tenure. To do the work that I do now while I was going up for tenure could have been career suicide. If you ask around your institution, you will likely hear examples of pre-tenure faculty members whose overemphasis on service unfortunately resulted in negative tenure votes. We do not have good data on this point, but I would wager that many faculty who do not receive tenure suffer from a lack of scholarly publishing. And while lack of scholarly publishing most usually causes a negative vote, I believe it often stems from spending too much time on service-related activities.

Service can and should be rewarding, but it should also support your teaching and research activities. As an academic citizen, you need to do your part to support the effective management and governance of your institution and discipline (Macfarlane, 2007). However, you must also remember that your role as a pre-tenure faculty member shapes the expectations and responsibilities you need to fulfill (Fairweather, 2002). In this chapter, I will discuss in detail the service-related activities that will prove beneficial and how you can utilize service in the proper context of pre-tenure activities. My hope is that you will not fall into the trap I did as an assistant professor, and that from day one you will focus on the aspects of your tenure case that are the most impactful. Yet, even if you find yourself now as an assistant professor who has taken on too much service, I encourage you to start approaching service differently. You can still adjust your career and ensure a successful tenure decision when the time comes.

TYPES OF SERVICE

In the context of tenure, there are two primary ways to categorize types of faculty service (Fear & Sandmann, 1995; O'Meara, Terosky, & Neumann, 2008; Ward, 2003). First, there are service activities that take place on campus at the departmental, school, or institutional level. These local activities tend to focus on operations necessary to getting things done on campus. Second, professional service activities include those with professional organizations, scholarly journals, and other activities that support the work of the discipline.

Institutional Service

As an assistant professor, you will likely avoid a significant number of institution-wide service activities. In most cases, tenured or not-tenure eligible faculty fill institutional service roles. While you may eventually be asked to take on an institutional committee after you have been on campus for several years and are approaching the tenure decision, I suspect most of your service work on campus will occur in your academic department primarily and in your school secondarily. There are a couple of reasons why pre-tenure service occurs mostly at the departmental level. First, as a new professor on campus, administrators and faculty leaders do not yet know you; this, practically speaking, results in a lower number of service requests. Second, most colleagues understand that tenure is your first priority and you have limited time for service. As a result, the time you do have for service will most likely be spent supporting the basic operations of your department, from admissions committees to student advising. Serving on Faculty Senate or on the institution's accreditation committee can wait until after you have received tenure.

Institutional service may take the form of anything from committee meetings with an ad hoc faculty group to deal with some issue in your department to regular standing committees for admissions or curriculum. In addition, you will be expected to attend regularly scheduled faculty meetings, monthly or less frequently depending on the department. In addition to committee work and meetings, institutional service also requires service with students, particularly if you teach undergraduates. You will receive many requests for letters of recom-mendation, or you may be asked to serve as an advisor for a student organization. Remember: At the end of the day, the primary purpose of institutional service is to keep the trains running on time. Someone needs to meet with prospective students, organize seminar series, help with assessment, and represent the department on the strategic planning committee. When I say that the tenure review committee expects you to be a team player, this is what I mean. Someone has to get the task done, and you can hope that senior colleagues will take on more than their fair share during your first two or three years. However, they may become frustrated if you fail to pick up any slack, and rightly so. You must complete your proportional part of service for your department. If you have 12 faculty members in your department, for example, you should do about 1/12 of the service in the department. Of course, this is not a perfect estimate. You might do a little less in your first couple of years, but do your portion of service— certainly no more and likely not dramatically less. Your department may help you by letting you take on easier assignments as well as those that dovetail with your teaching or research interests. If you are looking to hire a graduate research assistant for your lab, for example, you might serve on the admissions committee to get to know the potential candidates. But even when service requirements do not align with your other interests, you need to be a team player. Later in this chapter, I will offer more detailed advice for evaluating service opportunities. For now, understand that the smooth functioning of your department requires faculty service and that you will be expected to participate in at least some of this work.

Professional Service

For professional service, you will use your scholarly expertise to support the operations of your discipline in activities ranging from peer review to work with scholarly organizations. These entities require faculty to support their work, and ask them to serve as presidents, on awards committees, or chair sessions at professional meetings. Professional service, in particular, can significantly benefit your tenure case. It may support your scholarship or build a network of colleagues and institutions across the country. This can advance your career, helping you meet potential external reviewers or find research collaborators. A strong professional network also increases the visibility of your scholarly work and contributes to establishing your national reputation, a valuable currency in the tenure process.

Professional service typically occurs in two forums. Organizationally, the work of your discipline takes place in a scholarly professional association. You may become active within a broader discipline-based organization such as the American Sociological Association, the American Educational Research Association, or the American Chemical Society. Or you may find yourself in one or more specialized fields or disciplines that have their own associations. In either case, these professional associations will prove a significant vehicle for your professional service. Service in professional associations include opportunities such as serving in officer and board positions, joining association committees, and assisting with annual meetings as part of the program committee or in various smaller roles as part of a conference. Initially, you should strive to play minor roles in your association. As you move through your career, you can then take on larger, more time-consuming service activities.

Beyond service in professional associations, you will be called to share your expertise as a reviewer for journals, conferences, grants, and publishers. Peer review is vital to the academic publishing process and to improving the quality of work published (Lee, Sugimoto, Zhang, & Cronin, 2013). Reviewing can keep you up to date on recent research and trends in the field. Also, as top journals request your services, your reviewing activities can increasingly evidence your expertise. However, you must keep reviewing activities in check with your other responsibilities, as they can eat up time. And unlike departmental colleagues, editors have no idea about the other activities demanding your time. As a result, you alone are in the position to know if you can accept a review assignment or if you are overloaded and should decline it. In addition to reviewing responsibilities, you may serve on the editorial board of a journal in your field. The responsibilities of editorial boards vary tremendously by journal, but with a limited workload serving on one can help you learn about the work in your field and make connections with senior colleagues on the board. As you can see, professional service can often be tied to networking and publishing (Boice, 2000). Thus, this type of service not only benefits you by showcasing your active citizenship in your discipline, but it can also support your scholarly work.

Of course, there are other activities that may be considered service at your institution that also support your discipline and leverage your professional expertise. Consulting work, paid or unpaid, enables you to share your expertise with groups outside your institution. Some institutions actually have a separate category in the tenure dossier for consultancy, but otherwise work of this nature will likely be considered service work. Public education and sharing of expertise is another area of service. A scientist may visit a high school to share her research, for example, or a business professor may give a talk at a lunch about the state of the local economy; these are examples of how faculty share their scholarly expertise and experience with the public. These activities, although they may be related, do not fall neatly into teaching or research categories, and thus are typically considered service. Like most service, these activities, in appropriate moderation, can support the case for consideration as a strong, productive, well-rounded academic citizen.

DISPARITIES IN SERVICE BY GENDER AND RACE

Thus far, our discussion has not drawn distinctions between the varying service expectations, requests, and realities facing different faculty members. While service expectations and opportunities vary across institutions, research consistently finds that women and scholars of color face additional challenges related to career progression and service obligations (Eagan & Garvey, 2015; Hurtado, Eagan, Pryor, Whang, & Tran, 2012). O'Meara and colleagues (2017), in studying faculty using time-diary methods, found that female faculty spent more time on service, teaching, and advising, while male faculty spent more time on research. While such a trend can and does exist across all levels of academic

WORKSHEET 5.1 TYPES OF SERVICE ACTIVITIES

Begin by reviewing the vitas of faculty in your department or school who recently received tenure. Identify their service activities during their pre-tenure years. Write down each activity and note whether it is something you have completed, plan to complete, or will not complete prior to going up for tenure.

Institutional Service			
Activity	Completed	Plan to Complete	Will Not Complete
Professional Service			
Activity	Completed	Plan to Complete	Will Not Complete

careers, differential service in particular can pose additional challenges during the pre-tenure years.

You will not find formal policies around these issues in many cases, yet the reality of higher education today is that faculty members carry unequal service burdens. In their work, *The Politics of Survival in Academia: Narratives of Inequality, Resilience, and Success*, Jacobs, Cintron, and Canton (2002) described the unique challenges faced by faculty of color, particularly in predominantly white institutions. They articulated a "cultural taxation" that minority faculty confronted regarding institutional service. This term describes the often unrecognized and unspoken workload faculty of color tackle, serving as role models, mentors, and ethnic representatives. As a concrete example, institutions desire diverse search committees for new faculty. This means, given the smaller number of scholars of color on campus, minority faculty take on a much greater role in service to hiring committees than their white peers (Baez, 2000). Female students and students of color, as an additional example, often turn to female scholars and scholars of color in much higher proportion than male students to seek out support and mentorship from someone like them. The result is that these professors take on a much greater service role and, often to their detriment, one that is not formally calculated in the tenure process. While service itself does not receive much attention in the tenure review process, these important but small daily interactions with students and colleagues is certainly not viewed with the same gravitas as more formal service obligations, such as committee work. This results in minority faculty being hit twice, being asked to fill valuable but time-consuming roles as minority representatives and yet not receiving any credit in the tenure process for this work.

Research shows that female faculty typically take on a much larger role at home, which impacts their professional work (Misra, Lundquist, & Templer, 2012; Perna, 2001). And this translates to the academic home, as well. Research suggests that women engage in more service activities than their male counterparts (Curtis, 2005; Hart & Cress, 2008; Hurtado et al., 2012), and by far their service occurs in the realm of institutional rather than professional service. As discussed already, it is professional service more so than institutional service that can advance careers and improve tenure cases. If higher education systematically asks female professors to shoulder a bigger campus service burden than their male counterparts, it also establishes a pattern of work with dangerous implications for tenure, salary, and long-term career progression (Park, 1996; Winslow, 2010).

So, what does all this mean? First, all of us in higher education must acknowledge the inherent inequities by race and gender that exist related to service (Mitchell & Hesli, 2013; Winslow, 2010). Given that we know service plays a relatively small role in the tenure decision, we must also understand that inequities regarding service requests can negatively impact the long-term representation of diverse faculty among the tenured faculty ranks. Second, women

120

and scholars of color in the pre-tenure years must identify strong, supportive, and cognizant mentors to help guide service related choices and lend a hand protecting their valuable time for those activities most relevant to a successful tenure outcome. Moreover, mentors, administrators, and senior faculty must consider how and to whom service requests are made, and focus on the equitability of these requests. To the extent that a significant service inequality exists (Winslow, 2010), tenure committees must grapple with this knowledge in deliberations. Additionally, all of us tenured faculty and mentors of pre-tenure faculty need to stand up for our colleagues who face this challenge. One of the best ways to support women and scholars of color is to actively advocate for them throughout the tenure process and beyond. Finally, assistant professors must understand, and proactively respond to, race and gender imbalances to ensure that their careers are not limited. Women do not like service more than men do, and scholars of color do not like service more than their white peers. Yet, research shows that gender positively predicts the number and types of service requests faculty receive (O'Meara et al., 2017). Until these system-wide issues are addressed, women and scholars of color must protect their time fiercely—the repercussions of failing to do so can have grave consequences for a tenure case (Mitchell & Hesli, 2013; Rockquemore, 2010, 2015).

Such advice is not uncomplicated, however. As Pyke (2015) argued, the advice of telling individual faculty to "just say no" operates on a deficient model, that is to say faculty simply do not have the information or knowledge to manage their service obligations. Moreover, placing this responsibility on individuals ignores the complex structures and organizational barriers that produce institutional discrimination. In addition, asking pre-tenure faculty to personally manage the requests they receive does nothing to mitigate the inequity in how requests are made. O'Meara (2016) called on all academic administrators and tenured faculty to think critically about these issues, collect data outlining the prevalence of the problem, and work to remedy it through structural changes in their institutions. Workshops and training on implicit bias, discrimination, and other relevant research on faculty work can be a step in the right direction to address the complexities involved in differential faculty service. However, for faculty trying to navigate these issues on the tenure track, this can prove difficult, and you should seek help and guidance as much as you need. While I do not wish to promote this deficient discourse, I must also arm pre-tenure faculty for the current reality while working to change the broader context of faculty work. Understanding the imbalances that may occur in the amount of and types of service requests you will receive can help everyone make better decisions regarding service loads. If you are a pre-tenure woman or scholar of color, you may not be able to avoid inequitable requests. Yet, the burden for now is on you to guard your ability to focus on crafting a well-rounded tenure case, and to spend your time on the key priorities that will be considered by your tenure review committee.

Notwithstanding the absolutely correct critiques of placing the burden on individual faculty (Pyke, 2015), you have to consider when you should say "yes" to service and how you can say "no" in order to protect your time, focus, and attention across all areas of faculty work.

COLLEGIALITY

One of the most common buzzwords related to tenure is "collegiality"—and for good reason. Research has consistently shown that collegiality is the single most important factor in faculty retention and satisfaction. While not one of the three big tenure criteria—teaching, scholarship, service—collegiality nevertheless plays a significant role in tenure deliberations. At its simplest, collegiality describes how you interact and engage with colleagues. The term also connotes how you show respect to colleagues and act as a supportive co-worker (Cipriano & Buller, 2012). I discuss collegiality in this chapter because one of the most important ways you show it is through service. To be sure, collegiality can also come into play through your scholarship and teaching, since both involve, to some degree, interacting with colleagues. However, collegiality will mostly be discussed as part of your service activities.

Tenure committees of course evaluate your teaching, research, and service, but it is naïve to neglect the human element in these decisions. A positive vote for your tenure says that members of your committee would be happy having you as a colleague for the next 20, 30, or even 40 years. And no one wants to work with a jerk for the next 40 years. A department culture devoid of collegiality can increase faculty turnover, lower morale, and decrease productivity (Ambrose, 2005). So, at a human level, a positive tenure vote acknowledges that your colleagues feel they can work with you. While this certainly does not mean that you have to be the best of friends or even agree on every issue, it does mean your tenure committee will notice how you treat those around you. If you act like a jerk, it will simply be more difficult to vote positively for your tenure.

The problem is that, other than in cases of an obvious and agreed upon jerk, people vary in their definition of collegiality (Ambrose, 2005; Barnes, Agago, & Coombs, 1998). One of the contentions within this discussion in recent years is the role of civility in collegiality. Of course, I do not have to agree with, like, or want to spend time with a colleague outside of work in order to fulfill my faculty responsibilities. Civility is not identical to collegiality by any means. However, *in*civility can directly impact perceptions of your collegiality. If you act rudely, bully others, yell, or insult your colleagues, they will find you hard to work with. And committees will certainly find it challenging to vote for your tenure, especially considering all the privileges tenure entails, if your civility is questionable. Ultimately, civility can, and should, be considered as part of tenure candidacy, but tenure review committees must not make the decision overly personal.

I want to be clear on this point regarding civility and collegiality: I am not saying you cannot disagree with colleagues or advocate for your positions. As the Association of American University Professors states in their statement on collegiality,

> gadflies, critics of institutional practices or collegial norms, even the occasional malcontent, have all been known to play an invaluable and constructive role in the life of academic departments and institutions. They have sometimes proved collegial in the deepest and truest sense.
>
> (2016, p. 2)

The AAUP rightly cautions that collegiality should not render a faculty homogeneous. That pre-tenure faculty bring fresh ideas, new approaches, and alternative ways of thinking about academic work proves vital to a healthy and functioning academic department. Yet, some of these fresh ideas may clash with those of senior colleagues—or other disagreements may arise (Tierney & Rhoads, 1994). The goal of fostering collegiality should not eclipse or silence rigorous academic debate in a department. Rather, as the AAUP suggests, incivility in the more grievous form of "efforts to obstruct the ability of colleagues to carry out their normal functions, to engage in personal attacks, or to violate ethical standards" will negatively impact faculty evaluation.

As a pre-tenure faculty member, you simply cannot control the reactions to and perceptions of you by the senior colleagues in your department. Rather, you must treat all colleagues with appropriate consideration, respect, and open-mindedness. In my view, collegiality constitutes the heart of academic work. Everything we do as faculty requires collegiality—from research to teaching and, most certainly, service. While I am not arguing for a particular code of conduct for faculty behavior, it is nevertheless incumbent upon assistant professors to strive for collegiality given its role in the tenure review process. Personally, I was never very good at keeping my head down and staying silent in faculty meetings until I got tenure—common advice given to early career faculty. I understood the reasoning behind such advice, and I had colleagues who pursued more of this approach. Despite this, I believed that failing to speak up and share my views meant neglecting my duty to be a good colleague to my peers. You must decide for yourself how loud your voice will be in academic discussions in your department and beyond. Clearly, your context and placement in your department will have some bearing on this choice. From a tenure perspective, being vocal or disagreeable is not right or wrong, and it will not sink your tenure chances except in the rarest of circumstances. My advice to you is to disagree without being disagreeable. Without a doubt, I knew I had senior colleagues who disagreed with me on some major initiatives in my department when I went up for tenure. However, I also believe they understood that I was speaking from my convictions, that I had the interest of our department at heart, and they did not hold their disagreements against me. You must determine if the same is true in your department and respond accordingly.

As you can tell from this discussion, collegiality is another of those fuzzy criteria that impact the tenure process. You will likely not find it formalized in policy or discussed in specific terms. Like Justice Potter Stewart's classic definition of pornography, you know collegiality when you see it. In many ways, collegiality will frame the way the tenure review committee considers your case. Fundamentally, if your committee believes that you are a good colleague, they will be predisposed to support you. If they do not view you as evidencing collegiality, on the other hand, this does not mean that they will vote against you, but they may be less inclined to give the benefit of the doubt or support a marginal case. As you take on service roles during your pre-tenure years, always keep the notion of collegiality in the back of your mind. Doing so will help put your best foot forward and build up a foundation of good will from colleagues to support your tenure and promotion case.

WHEN TO SAY "YES" TO SERVICE

When it comes to service, the common advice is to listen to Nancy Reagan and "just say no." Since you first began hearing about service, I bet you have been told to be careful about taking on too much service prior to tenure. However, "just say no" is not very helpful advice (Pyke, 2015). To be certain, as I have argued throughout this chapter, you do have to limit your service and keep it from taking over your time and career. Yet, you cannot and should not avoid all service. Indeed, research suggests that faculty say "yes" to about three-fourths of the service requests they receive (O'Meara et al., 2017). Even if you could say no to all service requests, I would not recommend it. Instead, it is much more helpful to carefully consider which service obligations you should accept. Not only is "saying no" sometimes impossible, it also does not help you evaluate the myriad opportunities that will come your way during the pre-tenure years.

Compatibility with Teaching and Research

As discussed, service simply will not matter that much in your final tenure and promotion decision. Thus, the best service opportunities are those where you can leverage your teaching and research. Assuming you are at an institution where research constitutes the primary criterion for tenure, service that leverages your research interests is a must. From serving as a peer reviewer to joining an editorial board, this type of service can improve your scholarship while meeting service requirements.

Limited Time Commitments

When evaluating requests for institutional or discipline based service, try to seek out opportunities requiring a limited time commitment. For example, committee memberships with fixed term limits or work tied to a specific event have built-in stopping points to keep them from taking too much of your time. Similarly, service opportunities with limited scopes will get you involved without too much of a commitment. Before I went up for tenure, I chaired my department's fellowship committee. Each year, our department selected two doctoral students to be considered as university fellows. Our three-person committee had minimal responsibilities. We usually reviewed 8–10 fairly short applications and selected our two choices. As chair, I simply had to collect the applications, schedule a meeting, and write a paragraph about the merits of each of our two choices. It probably took four hours total, yet I got credit for chairing a department committee. If you are going to do service, better to take on a role like this than a committee with a heavy workload and meeting schedule.

Realize You Are Fresh Meat

As a new assistant professor in your department, you will attract students, faculty, and administrators. New students will see you as the new hip and energetic advisor for their ideas. Colleagues will see you as a potential ally for supporting their pet projects. Administrators will see you as open to new ideas beyond the cynical and stale colleagues who have been at the institution for a while. While you should avoid overly political and time-consuming opportunities, you will have the chance to engage in service work that can be rewarding and meaningful (Ward, 2003). As you evaluate the opportunities that come your way, consider those for which you alone are best suited. Ask yourself: If someone else had gotten the job over you, would they have received this request? If so, this is an opportunity you can safely pass up. But if the request is specific to you and your expertise, you may want to respond positively. Let's say a student asks you to serve on their dissertation committee. Does the student's topic fit with your research agenda? If so, it makes sense to say yes. But if you are simply fresh meat and the student thinks you will be easier to get on their committee because you do not seem as busy as the senior faculty, you should decline. This advice may not guide every request you receive, but it can prove useful for evaluating such requests, especially in your first few years on campus.

Bottom Line

You will inevitably have to say yes to some service opportunities, which makes the standard "just say no" advice not only unhelpful but also impractical. Each

125

TABLE 5.1 Service Obligations That Warrant Consideration

Service Obligations

Reviewing for top journals in your field

Reviewing articles related to your research agenda for major journals in your field

Serving as an officer or committee member for your professional scholarly association

Serving on an editorial board

Serving on a dissertation committee related to your research agenda

Serving on a department committee with a limited scope or workload

Guest lecturing on your scholarship

situation and request has nuance, and I recommend speaking with trusted colleagues and mentors about service requests when you are unsure of your response. Again, you must keep service obligations at a reasonable level and not let them take over your daily work. The table below provides some examples of requests that you should consider saying yes to during your pre-tenure years.

One final note about saying yes to service: I realize that some departments and institutions expect their pre-tenure faculty to take on a greater service role than what I have outlined here. Trust me, when I was undergoing the tenure process I took on more service than I should have. That being said, you alone retain control over your service work and the opportunities to which you say yes. While you may not be able to avoid service work as much as someone in another department or institution, you can focus on the principles I have described here to accept meaningful, productive service work. While you may not be able to escape a departmental expectation that you serve on three committees, you can at least say yes to those committees that involve lower amounts of work. In fact, a department that expects higher service loads requires even closer scrutiny in evaluating service opportunities. In the end, you will be the only one responsible for meeting all the obligations for tenure. Following these guidelines for saying yes can help keep your service bounded and contextualized so as to build a well-rounded tenure case.

SAYING "NO"—WELL

After you evaluate the service opportunities presented to you according to the principles noted in the previous section, you will undoubtedly find yourself having to say "no" to some service requests. For many faculty, particularly those who are pre-tenure, saying no can be incredibly difficult. You may feel political pressure to respond positively, or you may simply be a people pleaser. Either way, your tenure case will suffer if you cannot decline some requests that come your way. But saying no can also cause significant problems. First, you may say no badly. I will discuss in a moment how to say no well, but know that saying no in a way that insults, minimizes, or shows disinterest in the requester can cause problems. Second, you may mistakenly say "yes" to a request when you really want to say no, resulting in your agreement to do something you should not and do not want to do.

Before turning to the specifics of how to say no well, it is important to acknowledge the reality of saying no to someone. People on the receiving end of your "no" may be unhappy and not understand why you turned down their request. You must be okay with this. For causes both reasonable and unreasonable, some people will not appreciate being turned down. Remember that you cannot control this reaction, and giving in to it will only set you up for headaches and potential harm to your tenure. If you say no promptly and professionally, rest easy that you have fulfilled your responsibility to the person making the request. And while there will be people whose priorities differ from yours and cause you to second guess your decisions, you must not give in to the pressure from someone who does not like being told "no."

After deciding a request is not appropriate to pursue, provide a prompt, firm, and thoughtful response as to why you are turning it down. As we discussed in the teaching chapter, the best way to convey unwanted news is through the positive sandwich. In the case of turning down a service request, the positive sandwich achieves three goals: 1) thanks the requester and affirms the value of the request, 2) tells the person clearly that you are declining the request, and 3) offers a potential alternative resource. In practice, such a response looks something like this:

To: Rachel
From: Michael
RE: Curriculum committee

Hi Rachel, thank you for asking me to join the curriculum committee for the upcoming academic year. The work of the curriculum committee is critical to supporting the academic mission of our school.

    Unfortunately, in light of my other obligations at this time, I am unable to join the committee. In speaking with Daniel recently, he expressed interest in getting more involved in the school and may be interested in serving. [Alternative: I would be happy to share that you are looking for a new member of the curriculum committee at our next department faculty meeting if that would be helpful. Just let me know.]

    Thanks again for reaching out on this.

Best,

Michael

I begin by thanking the requester and affirming the importance of the committee. Then, I clearly state that I am unable to join this year. I end with recommending a resource of someone else who might be able to help or offering to spread the word that a committee member is needed. Note, I do not leave anything open-ended about my ability to join the committee. I firmly say no to the request. Additionally, I do not apologize for my inability to fulfill this request. You do not need to apologize for prioritizing your most important work and your goal of achieving tenure.

If you recall the weekly template we created in Chapter 2, your calendar can be enormously helpful in determining your priorities and declining requests. You have already set aside a certain amount of time for service in a given week; if those hours are booked, you should not take away time from your research or teaching but tell any service requester that your schedule is full and look for another time. Without this concrete sense of how you should be spending your time and with the deadline-free nature of much of your work, notably scholarship, service can easily overtake your time. A strong sense of priorities gives you confidence in saying no to service requests.

Until now, our discussion has focused on new service requests. Obviously, you should nip these in the bud prior to accepting them and realizing that you have overcommitted yourself. Yet, you may well find that you have already agreed to service responsibilities that are taking away from your other, more important work. What can you do in that case? I believe it is important to fulfill your commitments if you agreed to an obligation. However, that does not mean that you are stuck and have no recourse if you find yourself overcommitted. Instead, you should negotiate your way out of commitments when you realize that you are taking on too much or drifting too far from your key priorities. In consultation

---

PAUSE AND REFLECT

How do you usually say "no"?

_____

_____

_____

How can you improve your approach?

_____

_____

_____

with mentors and your department chair, identify service commitments from which you need to step back. Then, contact whoever is responsible for service work and have an honest, yet professional, conversation. The goal of this conversation is twofold. You obviously want to get out of your commitment, but you also want to communicate the advantage of your release to the person to whom you committed.

While this person may be sympathetic to your workload, the reality is that no one will like it if you dump work back on their plate. So, how do you do toe this line? First, avoid passing the buck with excuses like saying you failed to realize this obligation was going to take up so much time or that no one explained what was expected of you. Even if these are true, this statement will not help you negotiate. Begin instead by stating that you will do what you have agreed to but then explaining why this is not the best outcome for either party. Then, propose to help find an alternative to your participation. Here is a template using this approach:

To: Daniel
From: Michael
RE: Curriculum committee

Hi Daniel, I am writing regarding my membership on the curriculum committee this year. I want to begin by saying that I agreed to serve this year, and I am willing to fulfill that commitment.

However, I believe it would be in the best interest of the committee and myself for me to step away from the committee. The work is important, and I am not able to give it the attention it deserves at this time. I believe the committee would be best served by someone who is able to thoughtfully consider the issues facing us and provide better feedback to those coming before us.

With your agreement, I would like to work with you to identify someone else who could join the committee in my place and provide better expertise to the group. I have a couple of ideas and will remain on the committee until we identify a suitable replacement.

Thank you for your leadership of the curriculum committee.

Best,

Michael

In this request, I state my willingness to fulfill my commitment, suggest why it would be better for the committee if I were replaced, and offer to work to find a replacement. The request does not blame anyone, make excuses, or throw the problem onto someone else. I am offering to find a solution and to work on finding a replacement. It may seem easier in the moment to just quit the committee and walk away, but this will only hurt your reputation and leave your colleagues in a lurch. Even if that does not bother you, do you really want someone to tell the story of how you quit a committee and left everyone in a bind at your tenure review meeting? Following this alternative approach will take more time and attention, but it will still relieve you of your obligation while maintaining relationships.

Whether you are responding to a new request or seeking to get out of a prior commitment, saying no well will help keep your service obligations in check while maintaining positive relationships with colleagues. You will receive far more requests than you will be able to fulfill, so you need to practice declining some requests. Failure to decline well can materially hurt your tenure case by taking your time away from key priorities or by creating a reputation as someone who does not fulfill their commitments. Remember, time is a zero-sum game. If you say yes to service obligations when you should not, you will be taking time away from other professional or personal pursuits. Learning to say no well is one of the most valuable skills to master during your pre-tenure years.

PAUSE AND REFLECT

What service activities do you tend to say yes to that leads you to being overcommitted?

_____

_____

_____

When someone asks you to take on a service commitment, what is your first reaction? How should you consider adjusting this to keep your service load in the proper balance?

_____

_____

_____

THE DO'S AND DON'TS OF SERVICE

Throughout this chapter, I have discussed the variety of service opportunities available to pre-tenure faculty. Service is more likely to derail your case for tenure and promotion than tip the decision in your favor. Below are some do's and don'ts for service that can form the principles by which you decide which opportunities to take on versus those to turn down.

Do's

1. Do some service.
You cannot allow service to take an inordinate amount of time and attention from your teaching and research, yet you must do some service as a good academic citizen. When tenure reviewers see candidates who are not participating in service to their institution or their discipline, this can warn that they are disengaged or exclusively focused on their own work. At a basic level, tenure reviewers want faculty who will be good colleagues, and taking on at least some service activities shows that you are willing to be part of the team.

2. Do service that helps you meet people on your own and other campuses.
One of the rewards of service is getting to know colleagues on your own campus and across the country. As you prioritize service opportunities, focus on those that introduce you to people. The tenure process rewards faculty who are known as both individuals and experts. Service that allows you to meet colleagues, especially senior colleagues, can greatly benefit your tenure case. As an example, serving on the editorial board for a journal can count as service to your discipline, but it also allows you to meet senior colleagues who may later serve as external reviewers for your tenure case. Moreover, establishing connections with colleagues on your home campus, and other campuses, may open up opportunities, like research collaborations, that improve your tenure file.

3. Do seek out synergies with your teaching and research activities.
Since much of the tenure decision rests on your teaching and research activities, service opportunities that align with your teaching and research are win-wins. Not only do you get to check the box for service, but you also support your key pre-tenure priorities. Reviewing for a journal in your field is a good example of this type of synergy; reviewing manuscripts is considered service, but at the same time you can learn about current scholarship in your field.

4. Do let your chair or mentor be the bad guy.
Particularly early in your career, it can be quite difficult to tell someone no. You may be flattered by the request, feel the cause is important, or simply want the person to like you because they will vote on your tenure. No matter the reason, saying no can be hard. You want to be a good colleague and team player since you know this attribute's relevance to your tenure case. For all these reasons, I suggest you let your chair or a mentor be the bad guy. If someone asks you to take on a new service obligation, respond that you would like to think about the opportunity

and discuss it with your chair or mentor before accepting. After getting advice, you can respond that your chair has suggested you decline at this time. Even if you don't discuss the service with your chair or mentor, just putting some space between the request and your response can help you make a better decision. Ultimately, your chair and mentor want to support you and your tenure case. If that means they need to be the bad guy every now and then to help you avoid a service mistake, I suspect they will be more than willing to play this role.

Don'ts

1. Don't feel pressured to say yes or respond immediately.
When you receive a service request, it is human nature to want to respond right away. Moreover, if you are plagued by people pleasing tendencies, you will not only want to respond immediately but also accept the request. Then, after a day or two, you will feel guilty that you agreed to do something you really should not. When it comes to service, don't feel pressured to say yes or even respond immediately. Even if you end up agreeing to a request, you will feel better, make better decisions, and appear more thoughtful about your career if you take a few days to provide an answer. Most reasonable people will understand that you are in demand during your pre-tenure years, and that you must carefully consider a request before agreeing. If a requester is unreasonable about your need for time, you probably want to avoid working with them in the first place! Patience and pausing proves a real virtue here. Avoiding a knee-jerk reaction the instant you receive a request, which may end up costing you hours of time, will improve not only your chances for tenure but also your happiness at work.

2. Don't agree to committees requiring a lot of tedious work.
While you will probably never love serving on committees, not all committees are created equal. Some committees meet infrequently and do not require a lot of outside work, while others meet every other week with a stack of work between meetings. Curriculum committees are notorious for meeting frequently and having materials to read prior to meeting. I once served on my professional association's dissertation of the year committee. It was nice seeing the good work going on in the field, but it required hours of reading and commenting on dissertations. Needless to say, do your best to get on committees without these kinds of demands. The best committee I have ever served on was a career faculty award committee. We met once, reviewed the vitas of prospective candidates, discussed their relative merits, and finished within an hour. Best committee ever!

3. Don't accept too many manuscript reviews.
One of the most frequent errors assistant professors make in discipline-related service is reviewing too many manuscripts. It is flattering when a journal—

particularly a top journal in your field—asks you to review for them. In addition, manuscript reviews as I described earlier can blend your scholarship and service nicely. Yet, agreeing to review too often can limit your time and intellectual energy. Along the same lines, you cannot afford to spend days reviewing a manuscript. You certainly want to give it a thoughtful review and critique, but remember that you are the reviewer, not the author. Complete this task thoughtfully, but don't spend hours and hours on the review. Editors will understand that you can only commit to so many reviews at a time. When I was going up for tenure, I tried to do no more than four reviews per semester, a number I would recommend.

YOU CAN'T BE A HERO

If I can leave you with one mantra regarding service, it is this: Don't be a hero. For some faculty, service can be especially rewarding. I have often found this to be true of my service work both before and after tenure. Yet, you must remember that service, regardless of your institutional context, will not be the primary criteria for determining whether or not you receive tenure. Service can help your case and may well be required, but it is not the primary factor in faculty reward decisions about salary raises or tenure (Kasten, 1984). As a result, you have to keep your service obligations within the context of your tenure case. It can be tempting, when you see service work that needs to be done and no one steps up to help, to jump in to help your department, students, or others. These efforts may be appreciated, and sorely needed, but this does not mean that you must be the one to undertake them.

As someone predisposed to enjoy service work and who came up in a department that asked assistant professors to be heavily involved in service, I understand more than most the pressures to engage in service during the pre-tenure years. Yet, this does not mean you need to be your department's hero. While you may feel that you are helping your students or department by stepping into a large service role before tenure, the reality is you may be doing the opposite. If you take on a service role to the point that it harms your ability to get tenure, you are in fact doing your department a great disservice. As much as there may be an immediate need for someone to take on a service role, there is always more faculty work to do. Departments and students need someone to step up today, but there will be service needs over the next 10 or 20 years. If you do not get tenure, who will provide the leadership and service your department needs over the long haul? It may seem counterintuitive, but saying no and limiting your service before tenure is one of the best things you can do to be a good academic citizen early in your career.

That said, you do need to be a good academic citizen of your department and discipline through service (Macfarlane, 2007). As I have advised in this chapter, seek out service opportunities that leverage your teaching and research. Be a good team player so your colleagues will want to work with you for the long-term. Above all, do not be afraid to play a part in the intellectual life of your department, school, institution, and discipline. Engaging in service not only helps the governance of these groups, but it also helps you assume the role of a faculty member. Higher education depends on faculty members engaging in service. As an assistant professor, you must show an appropriate level of engagement to support your tenure case. Taking on the right level of service will not only better position you for tenure, but it can also establish you in your discipline and on your campus as a productive member of the academic community.

REFERENCES

Ambrose, S. (2005). A qualitative method for assessing faculty satisfaction. *Research in Higher Education, 46*(7), 803–830.

American Association of University Professors. (2016). *On collegiality as a criterion for faculty evaluation*. Washington, DC: American Association of University Professors.

Baez, B. (2000). Race-related service and faculty of color: Conceptualizing critical agency in academe. *Higher Education, 39*(3), 363–391.

Barnes, L. L. B., Agago, M. O., & Coombs, W. T. (1998). Effects of job-related stress on faculty intention to leave academia. *Research in Higher Education, 39*(4), 457–469.

Bensimon, E. M., Ward, K., & Sanders, K. (2000). *The department chair's role in developing new faculty into teachers and scholars*. Bolton, MA: Anker.

Boice, R. (2000). *Advice for new faculty members: Nihil nimus*. Needham Heights, MA: Allyn & Bacon.

Brew, A., Boud, D., Lucas, L., & Crawford, K. (2017). Academic artisans in the research university. *Higher Education*, 1–13.

Cipriano, R. E., & Buller, J. L. (2012). Rating faculty collegiality. *Change: The Magazine of Higher Learning, 44*(2), 45–48.

Curtis, J. (2005). Inequalities persist for women and non-tenure track faculty. *Academe, 91*(2), 21–30.

Eagan, K. J., & Garvey, J. C. (2015). Stressing out: Connecting race, gender, and stress with faculty productivity. *Journal of Higher Education, 86*(6), 923–954.

Fairweather, J. S. (2002). The mythologies of faculty productivity: Implications for institutional policy and decision making. *Journal of Higher Education, 73*(1), 26–48.

Fear, F. A., & Sandmann, L. R. (1995). Unpacking the service category: Reconceptualizing university outreach for the 21st century. *Continuing Higher Education Review, 59*(3), 110–122.

Finsen, L. (2002). Faculty as institutional citizens: Reconvening service and governance work. In L. A. McMillin & W. G. Berberet (Eds.), *The new academic compact:*

Revisioning the relationship between faculty and their institutions (pp. 61–86). Bolton, MA: Anker.

Hardre, P., Beesley, A. D., Miller, R. L., & Pace, T. M. (2011). Faculty motivation to do research: Across disciplines in research-extensive universities. *Journal of the Professoriate*, *5*(1), 35–69.

Hart, J. L., & Cress, C. M. (2008). Are women faculty just "worrywarts?" Accounting for gender differences in self-reported stress. *Journal of Human Behavior in the Social Environment*, *17*(1–2), 175–193.

Holland, B. (2016). Factors and strategies that influence faculty involvement in public service. *Journal of Higher Education Outreach and Engagement*, *20*(1), 63–72.

Hurtado, S., Eagan, K., Pryor, J. H., Whang, H., & Tran, S. (2012). Undergraduate teaching faculty: The 2010–2011 HERI faculty survey. University of California, Los Angeles, CA: Higher Education Research Institute.

Jacobs, L., Cintron, J., & Canton, C. E. (Eds.). (2002). *The politics of survival in academia: Narratives of inequality, resilience, and success*. Lanham, MD: Rowman & Littlefield.

Kasten, K. L. (1984). Tenure and merit pay as rewards for research, teaching, and service at a research university. *Journal of Higher Education*, *55*(4), 500–514.

Lawrence, J., Ott, M., & Bell, A. (2012). Faculty organizational commitment and citizenship. *Research in Higher Education*, *53*(3), 325–352.

Lee, C. J., Sugimoto, C. R., Zhang, G., & Cronin, B. (2013). Bias in peer review. *Journal of the Association for Information Science and Technology*, *64*(1), 2–17.

Macfarlane, B. (2007). *The academic citizen: The virtue of service in university life*. New York, NY: Routledge.

McMillin, L. A., & Berberet, W. G. (2002). *A new academic compact: Revisioning the relationship between faculty and their institutions*. Bolton, MA: Anker.

Misra, J., Lundquist, J. H., Holmes, E., & Agiomavritis, S. (2011). The ivory ceiling of service work. *Academe*, *97*(2), 22–26.

Misra, J., Lundquist, J. H., & Templer, A. (2012). Gender, work time, and care responsibilities among faculty. *Sociological Forum*, *27*(2), 300–323.

Mitchell, S. M., & Hesli, V. L. (2013). Women don't ask? Women don't say no? Bargaining and service in the political science profession. *Political Science and Politics*, *46*(2), 355–369.

Neumann, A., & Terosky, A. L. (2007). To give and to receive: Recently tenured professors' experiences of service in major research universities. *Journal of Higher Education*, *78*(3), 282–310.

O'Meara, K. (2007). Striving for what? Exploring the pursuit of prestige. In J. C. Smart (Ed.), *Higher education: Handbook of theory and research* (Vol. XXII, pp. 121–179). Dordrecht, the Netherlands: Springer.

O'Meara, K. (2010). Rewarding multiple forms of scholarship: Promotion and tenure. In H. Fitzgerald, C. Burack, & S. Seifer (Eds.), *Handbook of engaged scholarship*, *volume 1: Institutional change* (pp. 271–294). East Lansing, MI: Michigan State University Press.

O'Meara, K. (2016). Whose problem is it? Gender differences in faculty thinking about campus service. *Teachers College Record, 118*(8), 1–38.

O'Meara, K., Kuvaeva, A., Nyunt, G., Waugaman, C., & Jackson, R. (2017). Asked more often: Gender differences in faculty workload in research universities and the work interactions that shape them. *American Education Research Journal, 54*(6), 1–33.

O'Meara, K., Terosky, A. L., & Neumann, A. (2008). *Faculty careers and work lives: A professional growth perspective.* San Francisco, CA: Jossey-Bass.

Park, S. M. (1996). Research, teaching, and service: Why shouldn't women's work count? *Journal of Higher Education, 67*(1), 46–84.

Perna, L. W. (2001). The relationship between family responsibilities and employment status among college and university faculty. *Journal of Higher Education, 72*(5), 584–611.

Ponjuan, L., Conley, V. M., & Trower, C. A. (2011). Career stage differences in pre-tenure track faculty perceptions of professional and personal relationships with colleagues. *The Journal of Higher Education, 82*(3), 319–346.

Pyke, K. (2015). Faculty gender inequity and the "just say no" fairy tale. In K. De Welde & A. Stepnick (Eds.), *Disrupting the culture of silence* (pp. 83–95). Sterling, VA: Stylus.

Rockquemore, K. A. (2010, September 27). Just say no. *Inside Higher Ed.* Retrieved from www.insidehighered.com/advice/surviving/fall3

Rockquemore, K. A. (2015, April 8). Evaluating opportunities. *Inside Higher Ed.* Retrieved from www.insidehighered.com/advice/2015/04/08/essay-how-evaluate-oppor tunities-may-or-may-not-help-you-win-tenure

Tierney, W. G., & Rhoads, R. A. (1994). *Faculty socialization as cultural process: A mirror of institutional commitment.* Washington, DC: The George Washington University, School of Education and Human Development.

Ward, K. (2003). *Faculty service roles and the scholarship of engagement.* San Francisco, CA: Jossey-Bass.

Winslow, S. (2010). Gender inequality and time allocations among academic faculty. *Gender and Society, 24*(6), 769–793.

Part III

Arriving at the Destination

Chapter 6

Going Up for Tenure

Most pre-tenure candidates understand they must fulfill their teaching, research, and service obligations. You work hard for years to establish yourself as a strong candidate in order to receive tenure and promotion at the end of the probationary period. While we often discuss the broad criteria for the tenure and promotion decision, we give significantly less consideration to the actual process of going up for tenure. At the end of the day, your job as a tenure candidate is to portray your work during your pre-tenure years in the best light possible. You obviously need to conform to rules and guidelines—both written and unwritten—but now is the ultimate chance to showcase all your hard work from the last five or six years. Often, faculty work is isolated and little recognized; now, the time has finally arrived to demonstrate your value to the institution.

You must, therefore, make sure to document and present everything you have done in a way that provides your tenure review committees with plenty of evidence to support your case. Preparing to undergo a tenure review takes a lot of work, of course, but I actually found the experience cathartic after years of putting in my time. At last, I got to show off everything I had accomplished. In an appearance on the *Charlie Rose Show* in 2007, noted comedian, actor, and musician Steve Martin told aspiring performers, "Be so good they can't ignore you." In many ways, I believe this is how pre-tenure faculty should think about the tenure review process. Many academics are uncomfortable showcasing their work, but the tenure review process enables you to share all the time and energy you have put in, as well as your resulting accomplishments. Just as a good attorney would prepare meticulously to present evidence to a jury, you must craft a story, convey facts, and guide the reviewer toward the logical conclusion—a yes vote for your tenure and promotion.

THE TENURE DECISION PROCESS

The process to evaluate candidates for tenure and promotion is as varied as the number of colleges and universities (Goldsmith, Komlos, & Gold, 2001). Just as institutions value teaching, research, and service differently, promotion and tenure decisions are full of institutional nuance, historical quirks, and are derived, at least in part, from institutional cultural norms (Tierney & Rhoads, 1994). As with any other document you might write, you must consider the various audiences for your dossier. The dossier forms the primary text for the tenure decision at all levels of the review process, starting with your department and up through the institutional-level review by the provost, or perhaps the president (Bess & Dee, 2008). While you may assume your tenure case affects you alone, the reality is that its outcome reverberates well beyond you as an individual. Other pre-tenure faculty will look at your case as an example, just as you look at those who went up before you. Your department colleagues may gain a colleague for the next 30 years, or find themselves gearing up to search for your replacement. Your dean and department chair will face questions about their roles in developing faculty and providing mentoring if your case proves unsuccessful. Even beyond these stakeholders—and I certainly hope this is true for your situation—many other people are invested in your success and want to see you get tenure. All of them will watch your case closely.

While it is impossible to fully describe each variation of the tenure review process across all higher education institutions, there are some general parameters and levels of review that are found at most institutions. What I describe below are basic elements you will likely find at your institution, although you will inevitably find some variation within your actual experience. My hope is that this section provides you with a broad overview of what to expect and a framework to understand the particulars of your situation.

Department Level Review

The first step in the review process takes place in your academic department. A committee will either be created either specifically for your case, or your department will convene its standing tenure and promotion committee. This committee is comprised of tenured professors in the department, who may be drawn from all tenured faculty in the department, or from a smaller subset. They are the most likely to have knowledge of your areas of research and are familiar with your teaching. This is because faculty in your department are, in many ways, the most expert reviewers for your case. They have worked with you on committees and know you better than other colleagues on campus.

Despite this familiarity, be careful not to assume that faculty in your department are familiar with the details of your work. In academic work, we often do not know the specifics or, all too often, the bigger picture of our colleagues' work. For example, I may know that a colleague received a grant or is working on a series of papers on a specific subject. We may talk about how class went last week or discuss the outcome of the department scholarship committee meeting. Despite these interactions, I do not necessarily have the full picture of my colleagues' work, which spans all the areas from teaching to research to service.

Your department committee reviews your tenure dossier and discusses your strengths and weaknesses as a candidate. At the end of this discussion they likely vote, with each member voting yes or no to grant tenure and promotion to associate professor. Once the vote is complete, the chair of the committee drafts a letter conveying the outcome of the committee's review and vote regarding your candidacy. Following the department committee review, your case moves to the department chair, who will assess your case. In some cases, the chair's review stands apart from department review, while in other cases the department review gets incorporated into the chair's review. The chair then drafts a letter registering the departmental view of your case and his or her own vote before your file moves to the next level of review.

School Level Review

A committee of tenured faculty next review your dossier at the school level. This committee includes faculty from across the school who review all candidates up for tenure and promotion during that particular review cycle. It is quite likely that the faculty reviewing your dossier at the school level are not familiar with much of your work. For instance, if you're in a School of Arts and Sciences, the school-wide tenure committee represents a wide range of disciplines from biology to the humanities. Not only might the committee be unfamiliar with you personally, they may also work in disciplines quite different from yours. As a result, you must prepare your dossier materials to be understandable to educated readers from other disciplines. School-wide committees also have a number of dossiers to review, so you can significantly reduce their burden by following the guidelines for dossier preparation indicated by your institution. If committee members must read 12 dossiers, do not make them hunt through yours to find something because you neglected to follow the assigned format. Just as you may prefer organized student work when grading exams or papers, your reviewers appreciate anything you can do to make their jobs easier, and following set guidelines may help them evaluate your work favorably.

In many institutions, the school committee review operates independently from the department review to provide a "check and balance" for your evaluation; at other institutions, the school committee may be privy to the discussion and evaluation of your candidacy from the department level. In either case, the school level committee reviews your file, discusses the strength and weaknesses of your candidacy, and takes a vote regarding your tenure and promotion. Next, the committee chair drafts an evaluation report or letter summarizing the review discussion and vote outcome. This letter is then sent to the dean to be included in the dean level review.

Dean Level Review

Following completion of both department and school level reviews, the dean (and possibly an associate dean) review all materials related to your tenure case. These materials include your dossier and all previous reviews from the academic department, department chair, and school tenure committee. The dean considers all these evaluations and your materials before deciding to support your case or not. After making this decision, the dean drafts a letter summarizing his or her judgment and decision regarding your case. Depending on your institution, you may or may not receive the reports from the department and school level, but you should receive the letter from the dean regarding their decision. At this stage, all reviews in your school have been completed and your case moves to the institutional level review.

Institutional Level Review

The amount of review your case receives at the institutional level can vary tremendously, particularly depending on the size of your institution. Smaller institutions may provide more in-depth reviews at the institutional level, as they have fewer cases to review, while very large universities cannot possibly give all candidates a thorough evaluation. Reviews at the institutional level may include a faculty committee or senior members of the provost's office. The provost may be your final reviewer, or the president may take an active role—the latter being more common at smaller colleges. The description below details the most involved type of review at the institutional level. Your case may receive much less attention, but it will likely not receive more than what I describe here.

The institutional tenure and promotion committee includes tenured faculty representing the various colleges and schools on your campus. Since this committee also considers candidates going up for full professor, its membership may be restricted to full professors who can also review those cases. Similar to the school level review, you can predict that reviewers at the university level are unfamiliar with your discipline. Moreover, university committees often review every case on campus so their workload can be quite significant. At this point, in addition to your dossier, a number of letters have been included with your file from earlier levels of review, adding to the amount of reading required for your case. For this audience specifically, you must provide extensive evidence related to all aspects of tenure expectations. While you may rely on the fact that your department and maybe even your college or school colleagues know you are a good teacher, for example, there is no way you can expect your provost to know this.

Because of the range of disciplines it represents, the institutional committee often relies on your school's representative to provide context for your case. The primary purpose of this review is to advise the provost or president in making a final determination on your case. Different from the overly specific reviews you may receive at earlier levels, the institutional tenure and promotion committee often attempts to provide a fair and consistent review across all units on campus. As a result, this committee plays much more of a "check and balance" role to ensure that all policies and procedures have been followed as well as to evaluate the specific aspects of your case. After discussing your tenure case, the institutional level committee also drafts a report and takes a vote to support your candidacy or not. This report goes to the senior administrator who makes the final decision in your case.

While the Board of Trustees for your institution may have the final say in your tenure case, this level of review is most often perfunctory, a rubber-stamp for the recommendations of senior administrators (Euben, 2002). As a result, the decision of the provost or chief academic officer on campus constitutes the deciding vote in your tenure case. This person reviews all previous votes and evaluation reports, then makes a decision regarding your case. While they have access to your dossier, it is unlikely, given the time constraints and the number of candidates they must review, that they have the time or interest in exhaustively reading it except in the most controversial of cases. In most instances, the provost reviews all the votes and, assuming consistency across the various levels of review, makes a decision in line with earlier votes. For example, if the department, school, dean, and university committee support a candidate, a provost is highly unlikely to reject a candidate. Conversely, a candidate who has failed to receive support in earlier levels of review rarely sees the provost override such a consensus, absent a major breach of policy or some other major issue with the process. Upon making a determination the provost, or their designee, crafts a letter to you conveying their decision regarding your tenure case.

Tenure Appeals Process

Although you will not often need to utilize the tenure appeal process at your institution, you should understand your rights and the processes involved in appeal. Each institution differs to some degree on when and how you go about appealing an aspect of the tenure review process. Typically, there are three primary reasons a candidate may appeal a tenure review decision: The committee missed important evidence, you disagree with the committee's decision, or your institution's tenure and promotion policies have been violated.

If you believe a tenure review committee has missed important evidence or misstated facts, your institution should have a detailed process to respond. Spelled out in policy, you usually have a week or two to respond in writing to either the committee or to the next-level decision maker in the process (i.e., the dean). A standard policy allows you to respond in writing to the committee and identify the error or provide your counterargument. You may not be able to add evidence to rebut a claim, but you can at least state your case and perhaps ask for a reconsideration. There may be good reason to respond or appeal on the basis of missed evidence even if the committee's decision was in your favor. In this situation, you may still believe a committee's error could hurt your case in subsequent reviews. No matter the outcome, you can and should feel free to appeal or respond. However, I urge caution before doing so; you must seriously consider if a response is necessary. You may understandably be frustrated at this stage, but you do not want to appear nitpicky or petty. In the case of an egregious oversight—if, for example, the committee voted against your tenure because you had not submitted grants despite evidence in your dossier of grant submission—you can and should point to this evidence and ask the committee to reconsider their vote. But if the committee noted your 21 conference presentations when you actually had 22, and they voted unanimously for your tenure, you can let the mistake slide. If you do decide to respond, avoid an emotional tone and stick to the facts of the case. Avoid accusations and adversarial language. Show appreciation for the committee's time and effort through a factual tone that improves the likelihood of the committee favorably considering your appeal.

It is much more challenging when you disagree with the decision of the committee, not on factual grounds but in terms of how they interpreted your case. In this situation, the tenure committee or administrator presumably denied your tenure. Unlike when pointing to a specific error, as in the previous example, appealing a decision of how your tenure case was interpreted can be quite difficult. In this scenario, everyone agrees on the facts but disagrees on the outcome of the case. You are also hindered as a candidate, because you most often cannot access the external review letters that prove critically important. If you are appealing the decision on substance and not procedural grounds, seek to make a case based on the criteria in the tenure policies, and above all, respect the process. Try to describe, as clearly and objectively as possible, how you have come to a different interpretation of your file. Identify evidence from your dossier to support your view and seek guidance from a trusted mentor in crafting the letter.

Finally, you may need to appeal because you believe your institution's tenure policies have been violated. While hopefully such policies are not violated intentionally, if you have reason to believe they have been, for whatever reason, you should feel concerned and justified in your appeal. For instance, the tenure review committee membership may have not met policy requirements, or you may not have been allowed to include certain evidence that was permissible according to policy. The institution may have not solicited external review letters according to policy, or they may have failed to notify you of a decision in time to appeal properly. Or it may be the case that the tenure review committee was not internally consistent. That is, the reviews and advice conflict. For example, let's say that during the mid-tenure review the committee told a candidate to focus on journal articles and not book publishing. That same committee cannot turn around at the tenure review, then, and vote down a candidate for not publishing a book. Changing the rules of the game in this way can prove grounds for an appeal that may be more successful in terms of overturning a decision.

Regardless of the cause for your appeal, you must familiarize yourself with the process and follow the policy exactly. Candidates typically have a specific window of time to raise an appeal, and failing to respond in a timely fashion could cause you to lose your ability to appeal a decision. While you need to be timely, you would be wise to wait a few days before responding or submitting an appeal. Allow yourself some space to digest what has occurred, think through your options, and seek advice from mentors. As we discussed in Chapter 1, the tenure process is in part a legal one. You want to consider your options carefully, follow policy, and respond in writing.

Beyond the institutional level, candidates who are denied tenure sometimes take their institutions to court. Obviously, I am not a lawyer. You should seek legal advice before pursuing this path. What I can tell you is that there are two primary reasons faculty who are denied tenure seek relief from courts. First, they may argue that the decision making process was flawed. Second, they may argue they experienced some unlawful bias in their tenure denial. In a review of the case law, Kaplin and Lee (2007) suggested that these cases often do not work out well for the faculty. In the first instance, courts typically send the case back for a review without the procedural error, but this often still leads to a denial. For faculty who claim bias, only about 20 percent succeed on merit (Kaplin & Lee, 2007).

For pre-tenure faculty looking for legal relief, there are two significant difficulties in winning a court case. The tenure review process is inherently subjective, and courts are often reluctant to displace the judgment of university faculty and administrators. Moreover, the legal concept of academic custom and usage, sometimes referred to as "campus common law" (Kaplin & Lee, 2007), provides a framework to resolve uncertainty in policies or procedures. Academic custom and usage establishes expectations of academic community members for themselves and their institutions. Rather than courts making their own decisions regarding what they think is right or wrong, they often defer to academic custom and usage to determine a case's outcome or to resolve uncertainty. Ultimately, except in situations with clearly demonstrated unlawful bias, a court is unlikely to step in and order an institution to grant tenure.

TENURE REVIEWERS AS INVESTORS

Regardless of the audience, one way to conceptualize your dossier is as an information document for investors. Everyone voting on your tenure and promotion has a fiduciary responsibility to the institution to make the best decision possible. The decision to grant you tenure will literally cost the institution millions of dollars in salary and benefits over your career. You want to provide all the

145

evidence you possibly can to show that you are a good and, maybe more importantly, safe investment. Additionally, the more you progress through the tenure process, the more your reviewers will tend to be administrators. Obviously, every candidate would like a unanimous vote at every step of the process. During the course of the pre-tenure years, you hopefully developed a group of supporters and advocates to champion your tenure case through the various levels of review.

A natural part of any hierarchical process is that the first stages of review tend to determine the next. While the provost or dean has the power to overturn the decision made at the early levels of the review process, such a reversal becomes costlier the more overwhelming the earlier votes in your favor. If a tenure candidate has unanimous votes from the department faculty, the department chair, the school-wide tenure committee, and the dean, the provost may override the decision, but it will prove politically difficult. What this means for you as a candidate is that you should seek positive votes from the very beginning of your tenure review. The dossier is your best tool to demonstrate your positive contribution to the department, school, and university. It should convey everything that you have done across teaching, research, and service to meet and exceed tenure expectations. By identifying the most important criteria that will be used across the multiple levels and three main audiences for your dossier, you will position yourself to secure positive votes throughout the tenure review process.

THE TENURE REVIEW CRITERIA AND EVIDENCE

Before turning to the specifics of preparing the actual dossier document, it may be helpful to consider how tenure review committees, who review your dossier, evaluate tenure cases. If you have ever served on an admissions or search committee, you already have some idea how the tenure review committee process works. As with any group of people getting together to discuss an individual, the tenure review committee will have idiosyncrasies based on its individual members. Indeed, pre-tenure faculty often worry that tenure evaluations are based on subjective opinions of faculty work, particularly faculty researching in new and emerging fields (Austin & Rice, 1998; Delgado & Willaplando, 2002; Finkelstein & LaCelle-Peterson, 1992). Specific committee members may have personally preferred criteria, and may weigh the various aspects of a tenure case somewhat differently from other members. As with much of the tenure process, the particulars of your department, school, and institution come into play during these deliberations. At the end of the day, however, tenure review committees all look for a relatively similar set of criteria. For example, some committees may place more value on teaching, especially at institutions where teaching is critically important, while other committees, for example at research universities, may largely ignore teaching. While these criteria vary, you can reasonably expect committees to evaluate your dossier as detailed in the following discussion.

Your institution will require certain pieces of evidence as part of your dossier. Obviously, you must meet all these requirements and include all the evidence requested by your tenure guidelines. Nevertheless, you should consider these guidelines as minimum requirements, not the limit of the artifacts you can and should include to support your tenure case. If necessary, you should submit additional evidence to demonstrate your efforts across teaching, research, and service. In addition, institutions vary greatly in whether to include publications or evidence from your work prior to going on the tenure track, such as publications from graduate school. Some institutions require that you submit all your publications, even those completed off the tenure clock, while others only want to see publications from your probationary period. Learn the rules at your institution regarding the time period for including evidence within your dossier. The sections below provide some ideas regarding types of evidence you might include, and how different types can support your case. This list of ideas is not intended to be exhaustive. Instead, my goal is to provide you with ideas of the types of things you *may* include, rather than a specific checklist you *must* follow when preparing your dossier.

Scholarship and Academic Publishing

Tenure review committees want to see that you have produced the quality and quantity of research appropriate to your situation. They also want to see that you have gained at least some level of recognition for your work; this helps address the impact of your research activities. In reviewing your dossier, committee members consider the methodological rigor and quality of your scholarship as well as the outlets in which you have published this work. While committee members may not read every piece that you have written, you can expect them to be familiar with your work in terms of individual manuscripts as well as the total corpus of your published writings.

In addition to their independent assessments, the review committees rely heavily upon statements by external reviewers regarding your scholarship (if this proves to be a major component of tenure at your institution). For other institutions, especially those focused on teaching, external reviews may not be part of the process. Regardless at what level, the tenure committee looks for evidence that you have achieved a high level of scholarly success commensurate with your peers at similar points in their careers. You may find that your tenure policies refer to high-quality scholarship, expect outstanding research contributions, or utilize similar language. Ultimately, the tenure review committee looks for evidence in your dossier that you have become an established scholar in your discipline.

Types of Evidence

The scholarship section of the dossier provides evidence regarding your accomplishments as an academic. Frequently, this section begins with a brief discussion of your research agenda before turning to specific evidence regarding your scholarship. As you describe the elements of your research agenda, you should highlight specific publications that serve as key examples of your work. Use Worksheet 6.1 to identify the key strands of your research agenda and the exemplar publications for these strands.

Beyond discussing your research agenda, you may also include information regarding your publications such as journal attributes (i.e., impact factors or acceptance rates) or citation counts. As permitted by dossier guidelines, consider how to best present your scholarship and detail the impact of your work. You may list your publications by topic or chronologically. You could discuss each article at the same level or go more in depth on your most influential work. Your primary goal in the scholarship section is to help your reviewer understand your body of work as well as the significance and impact of your scholarly activities, which are significant to faculty evaluation at most institutions (Fairweather, 1996; Silverman, 1999).

Teaching

Your tenure review committees need evidence that you are a quality instructor (Seldin, Miller, & Seldin, 2010). Committees evaluate the teaching element of the dossier to see classroom competency sufficient to award tenure and promotion.

TABLE 6.1 Sources of Evidence for Scholarship

Statement of your research agenda

Copies of all publications

List of all conference presentations

Letters detailing grant awards

Reviews of your publications (i.e., review of your book)

Awards

Citation counts

Invitations to present your research

Media reports of your research

Confirmation notices regarding works in process (i.e., in-press publications)

WORKSHEET 6.1 DESCRIBING YOUR RESEARCH AGENDA

Strand 1.

_____

Publication 1.

_____

Publication 2.

_____

Publication 3.

_____

Strand 2.

_____

Publication 1.

_____

Publication 2.

_____

Publication 3.

_____

Strand 3 (if needed).

_____

Publication 1.

_____

Publication 2.

_____

Publication 3.

_____

WORKSHEET 6.2 DRAFTING THE TEACHING STATEMENT

Use the prompts below to develop the key components of your teaching statement.

Step 1. Write down your core beliefs about how students learn best in your discipline.

_____

_____

_____

_____

Step 2. Identify the content knowledge, skills, and beliefs that are important for students to learn in your discipline.

_____

_____

_____

_____

Step 3. Write down the ways your teaching helps students attain the knowledge described in Step 2.

_____

_____

_____

_____

Step 4. Describe the primary ways you assess whether your students are meeting your learning goals.

_____

_____

_____

_____

WORKSHEET 6.2 Continued

Step 5. Describe how you create an inclusive learning environment for all students.

_____

_____

_____

_____

Step 6. Identify the most specific evidence or examples from your classes that support the principles you have outlined above.

_____

_____

_____

_____

Step 7. Using Steps 1–5 as a guide, draft a narrative about your teaching beliefs, goals, and philosophy. Use the evidence from Step 6 to demonstrate the ways you successfully turn your beliefs, goals, and philosophy into your teaching practices.

_____

_____

_____

_____

_____

_____

_____

_____

_____

Committees want to see that you have taken your teaching responsibilities with appropriate seriousness and are fulfilling institutional expectations for faculty members (Eddy & Hart, 2012). Even in institutions that do not place a high value on teaching, review committees expect a basic level of competence best demonstrated by course evaluations, syllabi, documented efforts to improve curriculum, and other evidence of teaching (Arreola, 2000; Seldin, 1993). In a study of tenure dossiers at Cornell, Way (1992) found a tremendous range of evidence included by candidates, and similarly broad differences in how tenure cases were reviewed for teaching; this range demonstrates the challenges in meeting expectations in this area. At a minimum, review committees examine your teaching evaluations and expect your numeric scores to meet at least the department average and preferably be slightly above. The members may also look to your syllabi for evidence that you are teaching at an appropriate level of difficulty and sufficiently assessing your students. Your teaching statement or philosophy is another key piece of evidence that conveys your beliefs about teaching to the tenure review committees. You may have created this document when you applied for faculty jobs, but it is likely you have not returned to it since then. Spend some time thinking about the key elements of a teaching statement and compiling evidence of how you put your teaching philosophy into practice as you rewrite this important document.

If your institution places a high value on teaching, your dossier has a much higher burden to support your teaching case for tenure. In the same way that a reviewer looks at individual manuscripts as well as the body of your work as a scholar, your dossier needs to convey the quality of both your individual courses and the overall body of teaching work that you have done during the probationary period. To do this, you must provide the tenure review committees with plentiful evidence to support your case as a strong teacher who will continue to perform to a high standard when tenured.

Types of Evidence

Since the teaching section of your dossier must demonstrate the quality and effectiveness of your teaching activities, you should typically begin this section with a statement of your teaching philosophy before presenting evidence of your instructional activities, including sample syllabi or a list of courses you have taught during the probationary period (Korn, 2008; Seldin et al., 2010). You may not have given much thought to the teaching philosophy since you applied for faculty jobs. Even if you wrote a statement then, by this time you have developed a much better sense of your role as an instructor. In addition, you have built up a body of evidence regarding how you put your philosophy into practice. To this end, your teaching statement should not only offer your thoughts regarding how you approach teaching, but it should also incorporate examples from your classes

TABLE 6.2 Sources of Evidence for Teaching

Teaching philosophy

Sample syllabi

List of courses taught including number of students enrolled

Course evaluations

Peer observations

Examples of innovative teaching approaches (i.e., class activities, lesson plans)

Roles in curriculum changes and program/course development

Professional development activities

Laudatory notes or emails from students

List of master's theses or doctoral dissertations chaired and/or committees joined

of how you put these ideas into practice. At a minimum, your teaching philosophy should describe how you define teaching and learning, your expectations for yourself as an instructor as well as for your students, the primary teaching methods you employ, and how you evaluate student learning. Your institution may require evidence that does not fit well into a teaching statement, so you can include it in additional parts of the teaching section. Finally, you should include evidence of the steps you have taken to improve the quality of your teaching during your pre-tenure years. Describing these steps proves particularly important if you received low course evaluations at some point. Moreover, describing professional development that you have completed or other steps you have taken to improve your courses offers committees a positive perspective on even questionable teaching evidence.

Service

Tenure committees understand that assistant professors complete relatively limited service at this stage in their careers (Golde, 1999). Indeed, many pre-tenure faculty who thrive in their roles have been able to moderate their service obligations (Boice, 2000). Review committees generally consider service in two ways. First, they look to see whether a candidate has pulled his or her appropriate weight in institutional and disciplinary service. Second, they look to see whether a candidate has engaged in too much service resulting in a weaker overall dossier. For example, a candidate who completes less research than expected may have focused too much of his or her efforts on service responsibilities. In other words,

153

tenure review committees use evidence of service to contextualize the more heavily weighted research and teaching sections. Along these same lines, service can provide evidence of a candidate's activities in scholarship and teaching. Participating in a curriculum improvement process or reviewing for major journals in the discipline not only meets minimal service requirements, but also buttresses support for your case in the other two important criteria (scholarship and teaching). First and foremost, your goal in the service section of the dossier is to do no harm. However, the obvious secondary goal for your service is to support your case. Thus, you must portray your service activities in such a way that they meet the often decisive research and teaching requirements.

Types of Evidence

The service section of the dossier can be difficult to put together, as service often blends the two areas of scholarship and teaching. In fact, if you have followed my advice from Chapter 5, you have already accounted for most of your service work in these other areas. Does reviewing for a journal count as part of "scholarly activities" or service? Unless your institution provides clear guidelines—and many do not—you must make these judgments for yourself. Consulting the dossiers of successful candidates and discussing service descriptions with your department chair can help. In all cases, the service section should include governance activities like faculty committee work—on admissions or search committees, for example. You should also include service to your professional organization that is not specifically tied to research, such as serving on its membership committee. It can prove less clear whether to include activities like serving on editorial boards, reviewing for journals, or advising student organizations. In the absence of clear guidelines, I suggest conceptualizing these activities as service and, thus, including them in your list of service activities.

TABLE 6.3 Sources of Evidence for Service

Leadership roles (discipline, university, school, and department)

Letters of appointment to editorial boards

List of journals for which you serve as a reviewer

List of committee memberships with role (discipline, university, school, and department)

Paid/unpaid consultancies

Thank-you notes for completed service

List of other important professional activities

PREPARING THE DOSSIER

A dossier will no doubt fall short of expectations if it does not evidence the teaching, research, and service activities required during the pre-tenure years. Yet, candidates must spend time preparing the dossier in order to most effectively communicate the work they have done as assistant professors. The tenure dossier presents the faculty work completed during the probationary period. The term "dossier" is most commonly used, but the document may be referred to as the tenure portfolio, tenure file, or other similar terms. Once compiled in massive three-ring binders, many dossiers today are submitted electronically; despite this change in format, the central structure of the dossier endures to this day (Burnham, Hooper, & Wright, 2010; Danowitz, 2012). The dossier comprehensively documents all facets of the tenure case including teaching, research, grants, service, professional development, and previous tenure reviews (Lewis, 2004). The materials in the dossier serve as the primary evidence for reviewing a tenure case. Unfortunately, as has been discussed numerous times throughout this book, the same lack of transparency and potentially unclear guidelines that exist in the tenure process (O'Meara, 2002) also plague the preparation of the tenure dossier. Depending on your institution, you may need to compile an abbreviated version of the dossier for your mid-tenure review, and some of the following suggestions can help during the mid-tenure process as well.

In their exhaustive treatment of the tenure dossier, my former colleagues Joy Burnham, Lisa Hooper, and Vivian Wright (2010) found that, although colleges and universities offered directions and expectations regarding the preparation of the dossier, they did so with unsurprising and sometimes confusing variation. Some institutions offered specific guidelines or even checklists regarding ordering and formatting documents, scheduling appointments, and setting deadlines for candidates and review committees. At a minimum, colleges and universities tend to provide a baseline of the evidence to submit, although expectations can differ tremendously. Of course, one of the first steps in preparing the dossier is to get the latest copies of tenure policies and dossier guidelines for your institution (Lawhon & Ennis-Cole, 2004). Your department or school may have additional requirements, and you should seek these out as well. Read them in detail and ask senior faculty to clarify anything that is unclear.

In addition to reviewing relevant rules and policies, I highly recommend seeking out dossiers of faculty who have been recently tenured in your department or, if this information is not available at the department level, seek the dossier of someone recently tenured in your school (Bukalski, 2000; Gelmon & Agre-Kippenhan, 2002). Most newly tenured faculty, for whom the stress and anxiety of the tenure process is fresh, will readily allow you to see their materials and ask questions. When examining the dossier of a recently tenured colleague, look for two elements: First, review the entire dossier to get a feel for what is included

(Bukalski, 2000). How is evidence presented? How is the dossier organized? What aspects of the presentation seem particularly effective? Get an overall sense of the dossier so you understand how to present your case. Second, assess the dossier through the lens of the tenure policies and dossier guidelines you have gathered. Are there aspects of it that do not align with suggested guidelines? If so, seek clarification immediately, as you may unearth important unwritten rules. When I was preparing my own dossier, I reviewed the dossier of a faculty member who had recently secured tenure in my department. The first thing I noticed: Her document was much longer than 100 pages recommended in the written tenure policy. In fact, her dossier was almost three times as long! When I asked her about this discrepancy, she told me to ignore the page guidelines. Consider how critical this advice proved: If I never knew to disregard page guidelines, I could have severely limited the evidence I presented, sacrificing important information to adhere to rules no one cared about. Obviously, your institution should update policies and guidelines regularly to avoid this but, if it does not, you cannot risk missing a rule that is unwritten, that has changed over time, or that is not enforced.

The tenure years are often a lonely process of pursuing teaching, research, and service activities with limited feedback and an unclear sense of how well things are going. With the dossier, you have the opportunity to show off everything you have been working on during the pre-tenure years. In showcasing and presenting all of your efforts thus far, the last thing you want is to shortchange your dossier preparation in such a way that detracts from your accomplishments. While you may feel that preparing the dossier distracts from your work toward tenure, you must remember how critical the dossier is to the tenure decision process.

Preparing the dossier can prove time consuming, and you should allow approximately two to three months to complete it (Burnham et al., 2010). Of course, you must prepare the dossier well before the tenure review process actually begins. From your first day as an assistant professor, you must take steps to plan and organize the evidence you will need to include. We all know that trying to remember what happened last semester can be difficult. Trying to recall something that happened five years ago can be next to impossible (Whicker, Kronenfeld, & Strickland, 1993). Without documenting as you go and saving organized records, you will likely forget evidence you could use to support your case for tenure (Burnham et al., 2010). I recommend that all pre-tenure faculty create three formats of folders for dossier preparation: one electronic, one in email, and one in hard copy. Whenever you receive a document, email, or piece of evidence that might be used to support your case for tenure, place a copy of the artifact in its appropriate folder. For example, when I received a thank you note from a student, I put it in my hard copy folder. When I received an email from a colleague commending my work on a committee, I put it in an email folder. When the associate dean sent out a copy of the tenure promotion guidelines for the year, I saved an electronic copy. This will make it as easy as possible to keep track of important documents and mitigate the need to search for it years later. When it comes to tenure and promotion, strive for "pack rat" status, keeping anything that might remotely be of use when the time comes to put your dossier together.

One of the reasons it takes two to three months to put your dossier together is that you must balance content with presentation. Clearly, the content of your dossier constitutes the most important evidence used by tenure review committees in assessing your case. You want to include the best evidence possible and provide artifacts to support the claim that you have exceeded the criteria for tenure and promotion at your institution. However, remember that tenure review committees often review many candidates at the same time. Moreover, serving on a tenure committee is often a service activity your senior colleagues undertake above and beyond all of their other responsibilities. Anything you can do to facilitate their review of your work serves your case. What does this mean? First, the dossier should be prepared according to the guidelines for tenure dossiers at your institution. You cannot require reviewers to hunt for information; they should know exactly where to look in your dossier. Second, you must present your evidence as clearly, cleanly, and consistently as possible (Silverman, 1999). For instance, you should provide clean copies of your publications. No one likes reading low quality publications. Do the committee and yourself a favor and get clean copies of all publications and other materials to include in your dossier.

In addition, take some time to consider how to best present the various artifacts and evidence in the dossier. Your institution may provide guidelines to help with this, but it will often be left to you, the candidate, to determine how to make the best case possible throughout the dossier. Do you present your course evaluation scores in narrative form, in a table, or in some combination thereof? Do you list the committees on which you have served or provide a paragraph describing your committee roles? As you work through the various elements of your dossier, think about the argument you are making to your review committees and how you can make the best case possible for you and your work.

Remember, your institution has a deadline by when all materials must be submitted. This is a hard deadline; do not miss it. If you miss this deadline you risk annoying the tenure review committee—or worse. Often, these committees must complete their work in a finite window, and you simply cannot risk your case by submitting the dossier late. Dossier deadlines are frequently announced years in advance, so make accommodations to complete your dossier on time. I would suggest finalizing your dossier a week or two early to allow time for any last-minute finishing touches or to simply mitigate the anxiety of working right up until the deadline. Also, do not be afraid to ask for help from your department's administrative assistant or your graduate research assistant. You must complete some aspects of the dossier yourself, but seek help when possible to improve your efficiency and effectiveness. I strongly encourage you, though, to get personally involved in completing your dossier. Your professional future is at stake, and this is one area where micromanaging can be a good thing.

Personal Statement

The personal statement is one of the most important and influential ways for you to frame your case for tenure and promotion (Whicker et al., 1993). Often, you will provide your formal personal statement, or some modified version of it, to external reviewers along with some sample publications. The personal statement, at a minimum, describes your research and, more broadly, contextualizes your efforts within all aspects of your pre-tenure activities. After reviewing your personal statement, a reviewer should understand the background of your work. As a result, you should conceptualize all of the evidence in your dossier as your overall case for tenure. The personal statement is also the place for you to highlight your major accomplishments and contributions during your pre-tenure years. Not every reviewer will read all your tenure dossier in detail, but he or she will most likely read your personal statement. Highlighting your most important work in the statement provides at least one opportunity to make sure reviewers know about your major contributions.

One of the biggest challenges in preparing a personal statement is keeping in mind your multiple audiences with varying degrees of understanding of your discipline. Departmental colleagues and external reviewers have an in-depth understanding of your discipline and of the ideas you present in your statement. Reviewers at the college, school, and institutional level are more likely to have a limited understanding of the theory and methods common in your scholarship or at the outlets in which you publish (Silverman, 1999). This means you must balance writing your statement for experts in the field with writing for educated readers who may not be familiar with your field of study. Your statement should not undersell the complexity of your work, but it may require more explanation than what you might typically provide for readers in your discipline. One way to navigate this balancing act is to ask a few different people, within and outside of your discipline, to read your statement. Of course, having someone read your work is always a good idea, but it is necessary given the multiple audiences for your personal statement.

Another important role of the personal statement is to address any weaknesses in your tenure case. If you know an area of your case will prove problematic, you are much better off addressing this yourself and providing context to show how you have addressed the problem and worked to improve it. Let's take an example of overcommitting to service obligations during your first couple of years on the tenure clock. As a result, let's say you did not submit as many publications as you should have during this time. In your statement, you can address the problem, discuss how you have made changes with colleagues and mentors, and detail the efforts you've made to increase your publication output in recent years. Better to proactively acknowledge that your research output might be lower than you hoped and show how you have tried to fix this rather than to leave it to reviewers to draw their own, potentially more damaging, conclusions.

ROLE OF EXTERNAL REVIEWERS

As scholars, we quickly become accustomed to peer review. Journal articles, grant proposals, and most types of scholarly work undergo peer review. Peer review also plays a critical role in the final determination of tenure and promotion. Many institutions solicit reviews of tenure cases from senior scholars in the field (Schlozman, 1998; Schwartz & Schroeder, 1997; Yancey, Pitlick, & Woodyard, 2017). External reviewers play significant roles in the tenure decision, serving as voices of the discipline and attesting to your qualifications and success as a researcher. The internal committee reviews of your dossier rely on external letters as much as any other part of your tenure case (Goldsmith et al., 2001). As with letters of recommendation, you may not be able to see the letters of external reviewers. In rare situations, faculty union contracts enable candidates to view their review letters, revealing what external reviewers say about you. As a result, you should thoughtfully consider the external reviewer process and how to remove as much ambiguity as possible from the process.

During your first few years on the tenure clock, take the time to learn the rules, policies, and procedures for identifying and soliciting external review letters. Your institution's tenure policies will clearly establish the eligibility criteria for external reviewers (Gelmon & Agre-Kippenhan, 2002). In addition, you should discuss with your dean and department chair their expectations for external reviewer letters. Frequently, policies and eligibility criteria can help you identify reviewers for your case. Eligibility criteria often includes guidelines for reviewers:

- Employment at peer and aspirational institutions
- Academic rank
- Role as research collaborators
- Standing in the field

Tenure policies also delineate your role in the external reviewer selection process, which may range from identifying a list of certain reviewers, identifying reviewers who may not be contacted, or not identifying anyone (Seltzer, 2015). In most situations, you will be asked to submit a list of potential reviewers of your case. Your list then gets combined with one compiled by the institution (i.e., by your department chair or associate dean). Taken together, both lists are used to contact potential reviewers. Depending on your area of research, scholars in your field

159

may have significant intellectual disagreements. Your institution may allow you to identify reviewers that *should not* be considered because of bias they might bring to your research. For example, there may be a subset of your field that disagrees with a certain theoretical approach or does not believe in using a particular methodological technique. In these cases, reviewers who are part of this subset may object to your work for reasons other than its rigor or quality. Institutions recognize this, and because of this they often allow you to create a "blacklist" of sorts. Even if your institution does not have a formal policy for excluding reviewers, you may be able to discuss doing so with your department chair to ensure your reviewers speak to the quality of your work and not some other issue that exists in your field.

When it comes to identifying external reviewers to include on your list, consult widely with peers, senior scholars, and mentors. Faculty at your doctoral institution can also provide insight into selecting external reviewers (Burnham et al., 2010). Unless your field is very large, I suspect you will quite quickly identify reviewers that you want to include, as well as those you will exclude. In my own field, there are a handful of scholars who write harsh letters even when they ultimately support a candidate's tenure bid. In some cases, the stature of the reviewer may provide such benefit as to outweigh any negatives from a harsher letter depending on the philosophy of your institution. When pre-tenure faculty ask me about external letter writers, I warn about the reputation of these individuals so candidates can decide whether including this type of the letter— one that is harsh but eventually supportive—is a good idea or not in their situation.

External reviewers typically receive a cover letter from the dean or department chair, a copy of your curriculum vitae, a few sample publications, and your personal statement or another brief personal narrative (Goldsmith et al., 2001; Yancey et al., 2017). Based on these documents, their own experience, and their interactions with you, they draft a letter reviewing your qualifications, strengths, and weaknesses as a tenure candidate. External reviewers may comment on your teaching or service, but their primary focus is your research activity (Schwartz & Schroeder, 1997). Ultimately, external reviewers just do not have sufficient information to speak in-depth about more than your scholarship. Sometimes, your institution explicitly asks whether the reviewer believes you would receive tenure at their institution, but more commonly reviewers are simply asked to evaluate your case compared to other candidates at your level (Rhoades-Catanach & Stout, 2000). The answer to this question can prove the most important line of the external review letter. If a reviewer from a peer or aspirant institution states their opinion that you would get tenure there or that you are ahead of others at your career stage, this obviously speaks to your strengths as a candidate. If they, conversely, say that you would not get tenure at their institution or that you lag behind your peers, this undoubtedly hurts your tenure case.

WORKSHEET 6.3 IDENTIFYING EXTERNAL REVIEWERS

Step 1. Identify the criteria for external reviewers at your institution.

_____

_____

_____

_____

_____

Step 2. Brainstorm 5–8 potential external reviewers.

_____

_____

_____

_____

(from step 3) _____

_____

_____

_____

Step 3. As you learn of other potential reviewers during your pre-tenure years, add these to the list you started in Step 2.

Step 4. Discuss the names listed above with your department chair and mentors to determine their appropriateness for your institution, or whether they pose any particular problems.

_____

_____

_____

_____

_____

Since part of an external reviewer's evaluation is based on his or her experience with your work, it is important that you introduce senior scholars in your field to you and your scholarship. To do this, you need to participate in academic conferences and professional associations. You must also make contact with senior scholars regularly, asking them to advise you, to review manuscripts, and to discuss research opportunities. These interactions need not be elaborate; they could include simply meeting for coffee at a conference or sending an email asking about a recently published article. All of these interactions will help establish your reputation and help potential reviewers get to know you and your work. One helpful tip is to create a list of potential reviewers early on, based on your interactions with individuals in your field. If, for instance, you receive positive feedback from someone who would be eligible to serve as a tenure reviewer at a conference, note it so when it comes time to put your list together you remember that person. Early in my career, I created a simple spreadsheet with the names and contact information of people I thought might be potential external reviewers. As the time approached for me to create my final list, I reviewed this spreadsheet in consultation with trusted mentors. From 20 to 25 names, I narrowed it to five finalists whom I submitted to my dean.

As a final note, know that many institutions struggle to secure the requisite number of external reviewers for tenure cases today. With the faculty graying, service expectations increasing, and tenure-track positions declining (Altbach, 2016), this trend may very well continue. This could mean your institution actually needs more names than the policy requires you to submit. Consult with your dean's office and department chair first, but it may prove advantageous to include a supplemental list of individuals to serve as external reviewers. If nothing else, letting your department chair know that you have additional names should they be needed might even garner you a few more preferred external reviewers.

A FINAL NOTE

Beyond sharing all evidence of your accomplishments in scholarship, teaching, and service, your dossier must evidence how you responded to earlier tenure reviews. At a minimum, you received feedback during a mid-tenure review, but you hopefully received additional feedback regarding your tenure case from tenured colleagues, your department chair, and/or your dean. Document, for these audiences, how you responded to their earlier feedback. Just as you respond to the changes suggested by a reviewer when you revise a peer-reviewed journal article, you must respond to feedback from earlier in your tenure process. You may decide to do this explicitly by directly commenting on the feedback and what actions you took, or you may simply include evidence showing you did what was asked of you were someone to compare your work with the suggestions from prior reviews.

Of course, responding to feedback does not mean you have to incorporate every single piece of advice from earlier reviews, but you risk severely damaging your tenure case if you ignore it altogether. This feedback was hopefully designed to strengthen your case for tenure. As such, you should do your best to follow it. Even if you do not consider certain feedback all that helpful, tenure committee are made up of humans. If they took the time to review your file and offer feedback, they want to see you responding to their suggestions. In addition to everything else that the dossier conveys, it shows tenure reviewers that you took feedback seriously and responded appropriately. Demonstrating how you responded not only improves your case, it can also support an appeal in case you find yourself making one. Recall the previously discussed example of a tenure committee changing its mind mid-course on the importance of book publishing; if you have documented the earlier feedback not to publish a book, this will support your response of not focusing attention to this task. Ultimately, the tenure dossier presents your best case for why you should receive tenure and promotion and shares all your accomplishments and significant contributions across scholarship, teaching, and service. A well-crafted dossier makes your tenure case by crafting a narrative of your work and providing ample evidence that you have exceeded the institution's expectations for tenure and promotion.

REFERENCES

Altbach, P. G. (2016). Harsh realities: The professoriate in the twenty-first century. In M. N. Bastedo, P. G. Altbach, & P. J. Gumport (Eds.), *American higher education in the twenty-first century: Social, political, and economic challenges* (pp. 84–109). Baltimore, MD: Johns Hopkins University Press.

Arreola, R. A. (2000). *Developing a comprehensive faculty evaluation system.* Bolton, MA: Anker Publishing.

Austin, A. E., & Rice, E. (1998). Making tenure viable: Listening to early career faculty. *American Behavioral Scientist, 41*(5), 736–754.

Bess, J. L., & Dee, J. R. (2008). *Understanding college and university organization: Theories for effective policy and practice* (Vol. I). Sterling, VA: Stylus.

Boice, R. (2000). *Advice for new faculty members: Nihil nimus.* Needham Heights, MA: Allyn & Bacon.

Bukalski, P. (2000). *Guide to faculty advancement: Annual evaluation, promotion and tenure.* Los Angeles, CA: California State University at Los Angeles.

Burnham, J. J., Hooper, L. M., & Wright, V. H. (2010). *Tools for dossier success: A guide for promotion and tenure.* New York, NY: Routledge.

Charlie Rose Show. (2007). Steve Martin. Retrieved from https://charlierose.com/videos/20473

Danowitz, E. S. (2012). On the right track: Using ePortfolios as tenure files. *International Journal of ePortfolio, 2*(1), 113–124.

Delgado, B. D., & Willaplando, O. (2002). An apartheid of knowledge in academia: The struggle over the "legitimate" knowledge of faculty of color. *Equity & Excellence in Education, 35*(2), 169–180.

Eddy, P. L., & Hart, J. L. (2012). Faculty in the hinterlands: Cultural anticipation and cultural reality. *Higher Education, 63*(6), 751–769.

Euben, D. R. (2002). Tenure: Perspectives and challenges. Retrieved from www.aaup.org/issues/tenure/tenure-perspectives-and-challenges-2002

Fairweather, J. S. (1996). *Faculty work and public trust: Restoring the value of teaching and public service in American academic life.* Boston, MA: Allyn and Bacon.

Finkelstein, M. J., & LaCelle-Peterson, M. W. (1992). New and junior faculty: A review of the literature. In M. D. Sorcinelli & A. E. Austin (Eds.), *Developing new and junior faculty.* San Francisco, CA: Jossey-Bass.

Gelmon, S., & Agre-Kippenhan, S. (2002). Promotion, tenure, and the engaged scholar: Keeping the scholarship of engagement in the review process. *American Association of Higher Education Bulletin, 114*, 7–11.

Golde, C. (1999). After the offer, before the deal: Negotiating a first academic job. *Academe, 85*(1), 44–49.

Goldsmith, J. A., Komlos, J., & Gold, P. S. (2001). *The Chicago guide to your academic career: A portable mentor for scholars from gradute school through tenure.* Chicago, IL: The University of Chicago Press.

Kaplin, W., & Lee, B. (2007). *The Law of Higher Education* (Fourth ed.). San Francisco, CA: Jossey-Bass.

Korn, J. H. (2008). Beyond tenure: The teaching portfolio for reflection and change. In S. F. Davis & W. Buskist (Eds.), *The teaching of psychology: Essays in honor of Wilbert J. McKeachie and Charles L. Brewer* (pp. 203–213). Mahwah, NJ: Lawrence Erlbaum Associates.

Lawhon, T., & Ennis-Cole, D. L. (2004). Illuminating the path to promotion and tenure: Advice for new professors. *Journal of Faculty Development, 19*(3), 153–161.

Lewis, P. (2004). The publishing crisis and tenure criteria: An issue for research universities? *Profession*, 14–24.

O'Meara, K. (2002). Uncovering the values in faculty evaluation of service as scholarship. *Review of Higher Education, 54*(3), 57–80.

Rhoades-Catanach, S., & Stout, D. E. (2000). Current practices in the external peer review process for promotion and tenure decisions. *Journal of Accounting Education, 18*(3), 171–188.

Schlozman, K. L. (1998). External reviews in tenure and promotions decisions: How does the process work? How should it? *PS: Political Science and Politics, 31*(3), 623–630.

Schwartz, B. N., & Schroeder, R. G. (1997). External reviews: What is being done? *Journal of Accounting Education, 15*(4), 531–547.

Seldin, P. (1993). *Successful use of teaching portfolios*. Bolton, MA: Anker Publishing.

Seldin, P., Miller, J. E., & Seldin, C. A. (2010). *The teaching portfolio: A practical guide to improved performance and promotion/tenure decisions*. San Francisco, CA: Jossey-Bass.

Seltzer, R. (2015). *The coach's guide for women professors: Who want a successful career and well-balanced life*. Sterling, VA: Stylus Publishing.

Silverman, F. H. (1999). *Publishing for tenure and beyond*. Westport, CT: Praeger Publishers.

Tierney, W. G., & Rhoads, R. A. (1994). *Faculty socialization as cultural process: A mirror of institutional commitment*. Washington, DC: The George Washington University, School of Education and Human Development.

Way, D. (1992). What tenure files can reveal to us about evaluation of teaching practices: Implications for instructional/faculty developers. *To Improve the Academy*, *11*(1), 71–85.

Whicker, M. L., Kronenfeld, J. J., & Strickland, R. A. (1993). *Getting tenure*. Thousand Oaks, CA: Sage Publications.

Yancey, A. M., Pitlick, M., & Woodyard, J. L. (2017). Utilization of external reviews by colleges of pharmacy during the promotion and tenure process for pharmacy practice faculty. *Currents in Pharmacy Teaching and Learning*, *9*(2), 255–260.

165

Chapter 7

What's Next

On the television show *The West Wing*, President Josiah Bartlet was famous for saying, "What's next?" Bartlet's aides would often attempt to continue discussing some policy issue when the President was ready to move on and address the next topic. His go-to line, "What's next?" became a hallmark of the fast-paced nature of politics on the show. This question can be useful for conceptualizing the post-tenure years and "what's next" for your academic career. Assistant professors spend *years* preparing for a faculty career and doing everything necessary to achieve tenure. Now, you have achieved this goal. You have completed all the stages of the tenure review process, and you have been granted tenure and promoted to the rank of associate professor. This is a remarkable achievement that now puts you in a significant position to continue important academic work.

Before turning to what's next after tenure, I encourage you to pause and celebrate this enormous milestone. Very few people attain the title of tenured faculty member. This is the culmination of years of hard work, late nights, and sacrifice to achieve a major professional goal. The privileges you can now enjoy as a tenured faculty member will enable you to think about your career differently and prepare for the next stage of your academic life. In this chapter, I want to provide some thoughts from the far side of the tenure decision. My hope is that pre-tenure faculty can look forward to the career changes that come with tenure; these can hopefully serve as motivation to continue your push to reach the tenure milestone. Yet I would be remiss if I did not first emphasize the importance of celebrating the successful completion of the tenure process.

Upon hearing that their tenure has been approved, many newly minted tenured faculty feel a sense of anticlimactic relief. Everyone is happy to receive tenure— it is much better than the alternative, certainly—but the moment of decision itself can leave candidates feeling underwhelmed. For a few years after, when others asked what it was like to be tenured, I often joked that things had not changed much. After all, I still did my teaching, research, and service. As someone who felt free to openly share my opinions during my pre-tenure years, tenure did not change how often I spoke my mind or shared my views on departmental issues. Now, with the benefit of hindsight, I can indeed see the big and small ways that tenure changed my career. At the time, however, these changes were difficult to fully realize and appreciate.

Whether your tenure case sailed through or barely squeaked by, I suggest you take an opportunity to celebrate a successful tenure decision. Go on a nice vacation. Spend time with friends and family you may not have seen as often these last few years. Start a new hobby or do something nice for yourself. One of the realities of the tenure process is that much of your validation, at least professionally, is focused externally (Youn & Price, 2009). In many ways, your entire academic career relies on the external validation you receive from professors, dissertation committee members, or faculty search committees. Now, the ultimate validation has arrived in the form of a lifetime contract at your university. Naturally, newly tenured faculty may feel entrenched in this system of external validation and struggle to frame life after tenure (Rockquemore, 2016). However, that is a fight for the rest of your days. Today, find a nice beach or go to your happy place and reflect on the significance of what you have just accomplished.

My daughter, Rachel, started kindergarten the fall after I received tenure. A few weeks into the new school year, her teacher emailed asking for a volunteer to help the kids plant vegetables in the school garden. The kids would plant a vegetable, take care of it, and harvest it in a couple of months. As you can imagine, this teacher needed help wrangling all the kids. Before tenure, this is a request I would not have given much thought. After all, in my pre-tenure days I could not afford to take a few hours off during the week to do something like this. As I discussed in Chapter 2, I tried to prioritize my work during the week in order to spend time with my family at night and on weekends. After tenure, however, I felt like I could take the time to volunteer at Rachel's school.

In some ways, this may seem like an odd example, proving, perhaps, that faculty do not work as hard after tenure. I can hear the tenure critics now: "See, now that lazy faculty member feels like he does not have to work during the week after tenure!" But this simply is not true. I still ended up working the same number of hours in a week, but I found new time to volunteer at the school. I just woke up a little bit earlier on those days to get my work in on time. On the days I volunteered, I would write from home and use the trip to school as a much-needed break. The difference, post-tenure, is that I considered and accepted the request. Before tenure, my knee-jerk reaction would have been to not take on another activity during the day. After tenure, I was more open. Moreover, before tenure, I missed a few of Rachel's soccer practices and times that I might have helped her with her homework. Tenure provided the chance to get a little bit of that time back and rebalance my life. The flexibility of tenure allowed me to reconsider my priorities both professionally and personally. I not only joined projects that I would not have pursued before tenure, but I gave myself permission to use my time in more balanced ways across all areas of my life. The freedom and protections of tenure gave me permission to be more well-rounded, which ultimately made me more productive, creative, and, yes, happy.

WHAT HAPPENS IF YOU DON'T GET TENURE

Before discussing life after tenure in more detail, I want to briefly discuss an unfortunate situation that I hope you never have to face: What happens if you do not get tenure? After most cases of tenure denial, there is nothing else to be done and your career in your current institution will most likely end. Whether the decision was fair, whether you made appeals, or whether at the end of the day you know you did not do enough, the final decision has been rendered and you did not receive tenure. In many situations, institutional policy requires a candidate denied tenure to leave employment with the institution, particularly when moving into a non-tenure-track position or a staff position is not permissible.

After a tenure denial, candidates are often given a one-year terminal contract. Depending on individual circumstances, candidates may retain their previous responsibilities for that year, or their responsibilities may be modified. In any case, candidates should begin thinking about what comes after their one-year contract ends. Some candidates move to another institution in hopes of securing tenure there; this strategy is pursued—and successfully—by plenty of candidates following a negative vote. In other cases, candidates pursue other opportunities inside or outside of higher education. One question I encourage you to seriously reflect upon is why you were denied tenure. In many cases, tenure denials are rooted in a determination that the tenure-track position at the current institution is not the best fit for you. Maybe you enjoy teaching and service more than research, and you should consider tenure at an institution where teaching is prioritized. Maybe you do not enjoy the mix of faculty responsibilities like teaching, and you should look for a position that will allow you to be a full-time researcher. Discussing with friends, colleagues, and mentors about your best fit can help determine your next steps.

The most common reason for someone not receiving tenure is that their research does not meet the requirements at their current institution (Laden & Hagedorn, 2000). In some cases, this occurs because the current high research and prestige university only grants tenure to a very small number of faculty. In other contexts, for whatever reason, your record of scholarship simply falls short of the threshold for tenure in your current department. This does not mean you would not meet or even exceed expectations at another university or college. Over the years, I have had several friends and colleagues who, while unsuccessful at one institution, thrived elsewhere. A negative tenure vote is no doubt disappointing, and I hope you do not have to experience it, but it does not necessarily need to end your academic career. You might be surprised to learn how many faculty, considered quite successful today, did not receive tenure at

169

their first institution (Smith, 2013). In nearly all of these cases, however, these initially rejected candidates reflected on their goals and institutional fit and used this information to guide their next steps. I strongly encourage you to do the same to determine what's next for your professional future.

THINKING OUTSIDE THE BOX

Many faculty focused their pre-tenure years solely on meeting the obligations and expectations for tenure. As a result, they took teaching and research activities with an eye towards tenure, which likely meant making relatively safe choices. Research studies that might not have panned out, grant competitions with little chance for success, and innovative teaching approaches that may have fallen flat with students were all deemed too risky during the pre-tenure years. Now, after achieving tenure, I strongly encourage newly tenured faculty to shake off the reins and think outside the box. In an open letter published in the *Journal of Management Inquiry*, Corley (2010), argued that this transition represents an opportunity to do more than just add to the "I should" mentality that permeates pre-tenure life; rather, he claimed, it presents the opportunity to reexamine your career path and shift your orientation towards an "I want to" mindset. With that in mind, I challenge you to push your thinking about research, try new and innovative approaches to teaching, and approach academic work in newer, freer ways.

Understandably, many faculty hesitate to change the approach that led them to successfully achieve tenure. On the contrary, taking chances is precisely why the institution invests in faculty by granting tenure. Tenure provides the opportunity to try new things. As the number of tenure-track positions declines across higher education, these positions are evermore precious. Tenured faculty are entrusted with the privileges and responsibilities of tenure, as Rockquemore (2017) described it. In order that you can utilize this privilege and meet this responsibility, I want to push you to approach academic work in ways that are different from what you have done before. Adopt a way of thinking that asks how to try something in a more innovative way. Such an approach might not work, of course, and that is okay. Trying new approaches could also take your academic career to the next level.

Now is the time to do things differently. Curiosity and creativity are central to higher education, yet tenure restricts these values in both direct and indirect ways. As a tenured faculty member, you can now begin to think about leveraging your protections to foster creativity. This can occur in many different ways. Perhaps you will branch into a new research area or learn a new research method or technique. Or perhaps you will seek out a Fulbright award and take your work abroad. Maybe you will try a new pedagogical approach or teach a new elective. The opportunities and freedom after tenure are limitless, which has pros and cons. In order to think outside the box, first think about how the pursuit of tenure may have confined you.

PAUSE AND REFLECT

Describe 2–3 things you would have pursued during the past few years if it was not too risky before tenure:

_____

_____

_____

Now that tenure is behind you, brainstorm 1–2 areas you want to think outside the box:

_____

_____

_____

Ultimately, tenure means your institution trusts you to direct your own work. Sure, you will still undergo annual reviews or your institution may put you through a post-tenure review protocol of some kind. If your goal is to become a full professor, your faculty work in the future will undergo a rigorous review akin to the process you just completed. But generally, your institution will no longer look over your shoulder in the same manner as before tenure. While colleagues may have offered solicited or unsolicited advice about your work before tenure, you are now largely left to follow your own course. This can prove a freedom that very few faculty actually enjoy. Part-time and non-tenure eligible faculty must think about their next contract renewal. Pre-tenure faculty must keep their attention focused on tenure expectations. For you now, there are no such restrictions. Think about all the times you may have said that you would do something after you got tenure. Now is the time to put your money where your mouth is and follow through on those ideas. This may seem scary, but you never know which potentially risky idea may now grow into a career- or discipline-changing project.

In addition to the freedoms of tenure, you may also find that you receive more requests, particularly for service. This is not surprising, as studies have found that faculty members participate in more service after tenure than during their time on the tenure track (Neumann & Terosky, 2007). If you were protected from many of these requests before tenure, you may now be expected to take them on. You may also be asked to take on new teaching work and even administrative responsibilities. Without the wonderful excuse of working toward tenure, you may find yourself doing more of these activities—this is part of the normal career progression. However, you must also realize that these additional requests take time and energy away from pursuing new and innovative approaches to your academic work. As a result, you may encounter even more challenges to thinking outside the box. Just remember, you have more control over your career than you did before tenure. You get to establish your own priorities and direction. If you want to think outside the box, and I hope you do, then you will need to decide that innovative work will be a value for the next stage of your faculty career. It may be hard, but I absolutely believe that taking chances not only justifies your institution's commitment to you but keeps you invigorated as a teacher and scholar.

PAY IT FORWARD

Throughout the tenure process, you received help from many individuals. You may have received advice and guidance from trusted mentors, senior colleagues, or administrators. In addition, your colleagues may have taken on obligations to help relieve your burden during your pre-tenure years. They may have taken on a committee role so you did not have to, for example, or they may have taught a different class so you would not have too many new class preparations. While much of the tenure process requires individual work and effort, the reality is that many people supported you and assisted you in striving toward tenure. One of the best ways to acknowledge this support and show your appreciation is to pay it forward. Demonstrate how thankful you are by now supporting the pre-tenure faculty who come after you.

Especially as a recently tenured professor, you have valuable experience to share with pre-tenure colleagues. You understand in a real way the challenges they face, and you have recently survived the process. Thus, you are in a position to share your experiences and lessons from going up for tenure. From sharing your dossier materials to describing what your experience of the process was, you can provide valuable information to the pre-tenure faculty coming along after you. In addition, you can now ensure pre-tenure faculty have the support you did not during the tenure process (Bland, Taylor, Shollen, Weber-Main, & Mulcahy, 2009). As I stated in the chapter on service, I had a heavy service burden during my pre-tenure years. After tenure, I worked to improve my department's culture and decision-making processes so that we could expect less service from our assistant professors. I also accepted a role on a more time-consuming committee to free my pre-tenure colleagues from such a request. In large and small ways, as a newly tenured associate professor, you are in a unique position to support your pre-tenure colleagues.

A critical element of paying it forward is to advocate for pre-tenure faculty, specifically, and important needs in your department, generally. As you understand all too well, your power and influence can be limited as an assistant professor

---

PAUSE AND REFLECT

Which colleagues or mentors were most important to you during the pre-tenure years?

_____

_____

How did these supporters assist you?

_____

_____

What support did you *not* receive that would have been helpful to you?

_____

_____

How can you support those currently on the tenure track?

_____

_____

(Trower, 2012). Moreover, there are certain times when pre-tenure faculty do not feel comfortable speaking up. One of the most important roles for you as a tenured professor is as a voice in your department. You may have been more subdued as a pre-tenure faculty member, but now is the time to make your voice heard. By receiving tenure, you have been given enormous protections. Failing to advocate for important issues betrays some of the trust your institution has placed in you. Your department and your pre-tenure colleagues need you to take a stand on issues, including those that may conflict with your university's administration. As a tenured faculty member, you have been positioned strategically in your institution and you are part of a small percentage of people who are protected for voicing their views. Embrace this responsibility and serve as a leader for your department, school, institution, and discipline.

To conclude, do not think of tenure solely in terms of the freedom and privileges it provides you as faculty member. Rather, think of tenure in terms of the responsibility that has been granted to you. In an era where tenure-track faculty positions are steady declining (Kezar & Gehrke, 2014), you are positioned to lead at your institution as well as within your discipline. Students and colleagues will look to you, as a tenured faculty member, for guidance, support, and expertise regarding many issues. By successfully navigating the tenure process, you have demonstrated your readiness to take on this responsibility. You met the expectations for your institution and discipline by surviving what can be considered one of the longest job interviews in the history of professional work. For six years, you engaged in scholarship, teaching, and service. Your work was rigorously evaluated, and you have been considered to be among the top faculty in your field. I congratulate you on your success and look forward to seeing you work as a tenured faculty member. Your work in the past as well as in the future demonstrates and validates one of the most important distinctions granted in higher education: Tenure.

REFERENCES

Bland, C., Taylor, A. L., Shollen, S. L., Weber-Main, A. M., & Mulcahy, P. A. (2009). *Faculty success through mentoring: A guide for mentors, mentees, and leaders*. Lanham, MD: Rowman & Littlefield Publishers.

Corley, K. G. (2010). Letter from a newly tenured professor (A response to Hambrick and a call to action for my fellow associate professors). *Journal of Management Inquiry, 19*(4), 393–396.

Kezar, A., & Gehrke, S. (2014). Why are we hiring so many non-tenure-track faculty? *Liberal Education, 100*(1), 44–51.

Laden, B. V., & Hagedorn, L. S. (2000). Job satisfaction among faculty of color in academe: Individual survivors or institutional transformers. *New Directions for Institutional Research*, (105), 57–66.

Neumann, A., & Terosky, A. L. (2007). To give and to receive: Recently tenured professors' experiences of service in major research universities. *Journal of Higher Education, 78*(3), 282–310.

Rockquemore, K. A. (2016). Advice for the newly tenured. *Inside Higher Ed.* Retrieved from www.insidehighered.com/advice/2016/06/08/mistakes-newly-tenured-professors-can-make-essay

Rockquemore, K. A. (2017). What do you love. *Inside Higher Ed.* Retrieved from www.insidehighered.com/advice/2017/09/13/how-newly-tenured-faculty-members-can-determine-best-way-use-their-energy-gifts

Smith, A. (2013). Life after tenure denial. In D. Mack & E. D. Watson (Eds.), *Mentoring faculty of color: Essays on professional development and advancement in colleges and universities*. Jefferson, NC: McFarland & Company.

Trower, C. A. (2012). *Success on the tenure track: Five keys to faculty job satisfaction*. Baltimore, MD: Johns Hopkins University Press.

Youn, T., & Price, T. (2009). Learning from the experience of others: The evolution of faculty tenure and promotion rules in comprehensive institutions. *Journal of Higher Education, 80*(2), 204–237.

Index

176

179

183

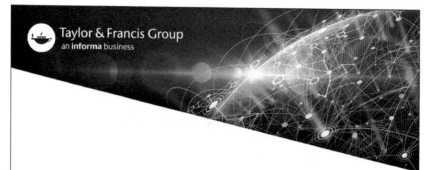